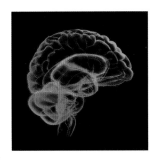

Deep Brain Learning

Pathways to Potential with Challenging Youth

Larry K. Brendtro, PhD

Martin L. Mitchell, EdD

Herman J. McCall, EdD

Copyright © 2009 by Circle of Courage Institute and Starr Commonwealth.
Published by Starr Commonwealth, Albion, Michigan.

For permissions and ordering including special discounts for bulk purchases, please contact Circle of Courage Institute, P.O. Box 57, 104 N. Main Street, Lennox, SD 57039 or call 1.888.647.2532 or 1.605.647.2532 or email courage@reclaiming.com.

ISBN 978-1-60725-789-9

Book design by BluFish Consulting, LLC, Marshall, Michigan.

Photography credits:

Page 8, Steve Liss, 2005.
Page 10, Helen Maczkowiack, 2006.
Page 18, Bruce Dale/National Geographic Image Collection.
Page 36, Gogtay et al., 2004. Copyright National Academy of Sciences USA.
Page 63, Steve Liss, 2005.
Page 98, Boys Town Hall of History Collection.
Page 116, Starr Commonwealth.
Page 126, Starr Commonwealth.

CONTENTS

Searching for Solutions

Nothing is as practical as a good theory.
- Kurt Lewin -

THIS BOOK SEEKS TO IDENTIFY POWERFUL UNIVERSAL PRINCIPLES FOR SUCCESS
WITH CHALLENGING CHILDREN AND YOUTH. Our discussion taps a growing
body of research drawn from diverse disciplines. This science is seasoned by the
practice wisdom of youth work pioneers, as well as our own experience building
educational and treatment programs at Starr Commonwealth in Michigan and
Ohio. During the decades we have been in this field, research on troubled
children has mushroomed but the quality of practice has often declined. Our
goal is to provide a roadmap to powerful educational and treatment strategies
that enable youth to transform their troubled lives.

Enduring Truths

A century ago, Ellen Key noted that enduring truths must be rediscovered
by each new generation.[1] Few are aware of the rich tradition of ideas put forth
by early leaders in work with children in conflict. Nor are they able to sort
out truth from trivia in the glut of publications that can even overwhelm
the most serious scholar.

More research does not necessarily lead to more truth. In 1800, there
were but 1000 persons in the world who might be considered scientists.
Two centuries later, millions are churning out mountains of research reports.
Most are wrong, and even studies that are technically accurate seldom
apply to real-world problems.[2]

It may be helpful to get our bearings by revisiting enduring truths
put forth by the earliest pioneers in this field. The first widely circulated scientific

reports of work with troubled children date back to the beginning of the nineteenth century. Most prominent are the writings of Swiss educator Johann Pestalozzi and French physician Jean Marc Itard.

In 1801, Pestalozzi created a stir across Europe by describing how children from very deprived backgrounds could be educated and reclaimed as solid citizens.[3] He developed these ideas in residential schools he founded for cast-off children who roamed the streets of European cities after the Napoleonic wars. Pestalozzi created sophisticated pedagogical techniques, but he concluded that the ultimate goal of education was to create a moral individual. He showed that relationships of love, trust, and gratitude provided the key to success with challenging children and youth.[4] Pestalozzi's ideas became a beacon to guide progressive theories of education and treatment.

Itard described the education and treatment of *The Wild Boy of Averyon*[5] which was also published in 1801. This youth, whom he named Victor, had been physically abused and abandoned and had to forage nude in the woods of the French highlands. When lured into human contact, he was mute, animal-like, and seemed to lack human empathy. Over a period of years, Itard was able to rekindle human attachment but Victor never developed verbal language. This study is seen as the first carefully documented account of an autistic child. Itard concluded that "to be judged fairly, this young man must be compared only to himself."[6] Modern schemes of bell-curve testing and deficit-based diagnosis have strayed far from this standard.

Flawed Theories

To transpose Lewin's truism, nothing is as useless as a flawed theory. In their book on the neuroscience of love, psychiatrists Thomas Lewis, Fari Amini, and Richard Lannon describe how various models of psychology present distorted images of human behavior:

- Psychoanalysis got sidetracked studying sexual urges, and "efficacy was not among the model's advantage."[7]

- Behaviorism brandished empiricism but was discredited by its ignorance of "such staples of human life as thought or desire."[8]
- Cognitive psychology bristled with boxes and arrows but left out "the unthinking center of self that people most cherish."[9]
- Drugs, prescribed or otherwise, fail to heal human "isolation, sorrow, bitterness, anxiety, loneliness, and despair."[10]
- Evolutionary psychology dismissed "kindness, religion, art, music, and poetry" as illusions without survival value.[11]

In similar manner, many modern schools have mutated into giant test prep centers, following a sterile curriculum that fails to engage students.[12] Zero tolerance discipline policies exclude or expel youngsters with emotional and behavioral problems.[13] Those who run afoul of the law are often discarded in punitive correctional systems that fail to redeem these most needy young persons.[14]

When formal theories don't fit real world problems, humans revert to *naïve psychology* and operate on folk theories of behavior.[15] A major study of public school programs for troubled children by our mentor, William Morse, found that educators without a clear theory used *green thumb* or *primitive* approaches.[16] A prominent child psychiatrist suggested that his profession also lacks a unifying theory, so many practitioners revert to *whatever works*.[17]

Missing from most current theories are the voices of youth. James Anglin of the University of Victoria conducted research with troubled youth and their staff in ten Canadian group care facilities.[18] He was surprised to find that the four-letter word that young people most often used to describe their experience was PAIN. All spoke of deep emotional distress in their lives. Yet descriptions by staff used labels like *disruptive* or *behaviorally disordered*. Anglin suggests a more accurate description would be *pain-based behavior*.

While kids and families may be in pain, prevailing rhetoric tilts towards youth bashing and parent blaming. As with sneaky political spin, it is hard to spot biased language which subtly demeans and dehumanizes.[19] Why is it fair for professionals to use the term *dysfunctional family* unless the term *dysfunctional professional* is also acceptable in common usage? Similarly, we have chosen to use the term *antisocial* only to describe behavior, not to label youth in conflict. Most of these kids are very social, just not with us. Further, those who show antisocial behavior have often been neglected or maltreated by adults and institutions responsible for their socialization. It might be more accurate to label the schools and correctional programs which discard kids as *antisocial*.

Success with challenging youth requires that we break free from folk psychology and narrow theories of behavior. Only then can we *respond to the needs* of youth instead of *react to their problems*.[20] What is required is a new approach that links together research, practice, and deep values of mutual respect. Philosophers of science have a name for this integration of knowledge: *consilience*.

The Test for Truth

The gold standard for truth is that an idea from one field fits with ideas drawn from other realms of experience. This was called *consilience* by William Whewell, a nineteenth century English wordsmith who also invented the term *scientist*.[21] Trained in architecture, theology, and science, he was intrigued to discover connections between these dissimilar disciplines.

The belief that all knowledge is related dates back to the earliest universities. An educated person was expected to master the *liberal arts* including the natural sciences, social sciences, and humanities. The word *college* originally referred to *colleagues* who joined together to share their scholarship. But as scholars focused on increasingly narrow areas of expertise, the idea of consilience was largely forgotten.

The call for consilience has been renewed by Harvard biologist Edward O. Wilson who believes that modern science has become captive to its own complexity. Universities chop up knowledge into "a flurry of minor disciplines and specialized courses" and lose sight of the big truths.[22] Consilience links findings from separate fields to discover simpler universal principles. Simple does not mean simplistic, since basic truths can be profound. In fact, Einstein suggested that if you can't explain your theory to a six year old, you probably do not understand it yourself.

Truth cannot contradict truth, declared Pope John Paul II as he worked to build bridges between scientific and spiritual world-views.[23] Consilience requires that truth be tested against multiple perspectives of science, practice wisdom, and universal human values.

The accompanying figure shows how consilience is achieved. We are most likely to solve challenging real-world problems by tapping ideas that overlap at the center of the circle. When everything *clicks* and *falls in place*, we are one step closer to the truth.

The human brain is designed to make new connections between ideas, which is called the *Aha* or *Eureka* experience.[24] It is as if a light bulb turns on and we suddenly find a fresh answer to a problem that long eluded us. At these flashes of discovery, separate ideas jump together, to use Whewell's words. To reward us for our brilliance, the brain spikes a rush of pleasure chemicals.

Many creative solutions connect separate, simpler ideas. An example was shared by Brian, a youth hired for a routine job in a *star wars* research lab. Engineers stumped by a mechanical problem proposed designing a new component costing thousands of dollars. Brian tapped his hobby of repairing cars to find a simple solution inspired by a carburetor mechanism from his Dad's old pickup.

Success with challenging youth requires all the knowledge we can muster. When we tap varied perspectives, the big picture becomes clear. For example, note the consilience in these four views about the essential needs of children and youth:

- BIOLOGICAL SCIENCE reveals that brains of children have inbuilt attachment programs which strongly motivate them to seek out positive bonds with caring adults.

- SOCIAL SCIENCE shows that democratic leadership creates cooperative climates among youth and adults, while permissive or autocratic approaches fuel chaos or rebellion.

- PRACTICE EXPERTISE from successful experience and the collective wisdom of youth work pioneers demonstrates the restorative power of human relationships.

- VALUES of human dignity motivate us to create caring environments where all young persons are treated with respect.

Twisting the Truth

The human brain likes all of its ideas to hang together, even if this means distorting the truth to keep beliefs consistent. If some idea does not fit, this creates what Leon Festinger called cognitive dissonance. Our befuddled brain tries to get thinking back in balance, even by ignoring truth or embracing lies.[25] Ideas that fit together seem to make sense to the brain, even if profoundly wrong. Below are examples of distortions of truth, drawn from our participation in Institutes for Healing Racism.

- BIASED BIOLOGICAL SCIENCE spreads the faulty theory that there are separate races of humanity and some are superior.

- BIASED SOCIAL SCIENCE invents "cultural deprivation" to promote assimilation of indigenous nations and other minorities.

- COERCIVE PRACTICES produce schools and curriculums that discount non-mainstream values and foster White privilege.

- DEHUMANIZING VALUES contradict human dignity and justify segregation and discrimination against certain populations.

Should an individual espouse such beliefs, this might be ignorance. But when such fallacies become enshrined in policy and practice, this has escalated into political and system abuse.[26]

Many popular approaches to education, treatment, and juvenile justice are devoid of any scientific rationale but still have enthusiastic proponents. Hundreds of *violence prevention* and *character education* schemes promise panaceas to scary problems. For-profit boot camps spirit away troubled teens from families who are desperate for solutions. People may strongly cling to such approaches, even in the absence of any solid evidence.

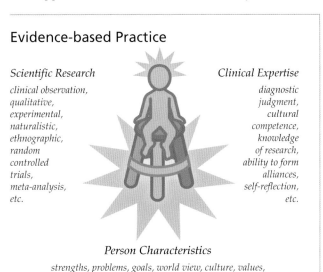

Evidence-based Practice

Scientific Research

clinical observation, qualitative, experimental, naturalistic, ethnographic, random controlled trials, meta-analysis, etc.

Clinical Expertise

diagnostic judgment, cultural competence, knowledge of research, ability to form alliances, self-reflection, etc.

Person Characteristics

strengths, problems, goals, world view, culture, values, developmental history, personal ecology, etc.

Even when programs claim to be *evidence-based*, this may mean little, since Googling those buzz words turns up ten million hits. Some argue that the *gold standard* for evaluating effectiveness requires random clinical trials as used by the drug industry – as if this inspires much credibility. What we really need are scientific methods matched to the practical challenges of changing young lives.[27]

The best current definition of evidence-based practice comes from the American Psychological Association.[28] As shown by the three-legged stool in the accompanying illustration, knowledge about the *individual* must be balanced with *practice expertise* and *research* from multiple perspectives. This definition is a solid example of consilience because it triangulates evidence from various sources.

Unfortunately, much discussion of so-called evidence-based approaches is simplistic and sometimes deceptive, driven by politics or profits. Slick science is at the service of corporations selling drugs as the solution to problems in living. Program evaluators may have conflicts of interest motivating them to produce glowing reports of mundane methods. Government agencies create blue ribbon lists of approved programs which become a passport to funding, but shallow qualifications for inclusion contradict the standard of consilience.

For over twenty years, Bessel van der Kolk has been on the forefront of researching effective interventions with persons in conflict. He strongly opposes anointing certain methods as *evidence-based* merely because they prevail in narrow comparative studies. van der Kolk contends that passing out seals of approval as *treatments of choice* violates the spirit of science:

> This concern is particularly relevant as long as the findings of neuroscience, attachment, and cross-cultural research remain isolated from an increasingly prescriptive approach to intervention and treatment.[29]

The Big Picture

The best exemplar of consilience in programs for children and youth is the *bioecological* model developed across six decades by Urie Bronfenbrenner of Cornell University.[30] He described traditional psychological research as the study of "the strange behavior of children in strange situations with strange adults for the briefest possible periods of time."[31] He scoffed at the notion that solid research meant random assignment to controlled situations or other narrow methods. The bioecological model is the most extensively researched approach to understanding child and youth development.

Bronfenbrenner's most basic belief was that trusting bonds with children are the most powerful force in building healthy brains and behavior. He translated this principle in simple but powerful terms: Every child needs at least one adult who is irrationally crazy about him or her.[32] Young people thrive in ecologies with caring families, concerned teachers, positive peers, and a supportive community. But children reared in unhealthy ecologies experience a host of emotional, behavioral, and learning problems.

Instead of diagnosing these as pathology or disease in the person, Bronfenbrenner focused on DIS-EASE in the ecology.

The Ecology of Childhood

The key circles of influence in the child's life space are shown in the accompanying figure.[33] The most powerful circles make up the immediate life space of family, school, peer group, and community connections like work, church, and youth organizations. Enmeshed in this ecology, a child with a unique biological and psychological makeup interacts with significant others. Surrounding this immediate life space are broader circles of influence including cultural, economic, and political forces.[34]

A child's immediate life space wields more clout than the broad ecology. The most potent forces come from the micro ecology, namely, what happens in one's own home, peer group, school, and neighborhood. A disrupted community ecology can be offset by strong parental influence. Contrary to stereotypes, many low income urban families have strengths to offset risk and are skilled in meeting their children's needs.[35] But when families are vulnerable, supports from other areas of the ecology are critically important. Past and current problems need not predict future fate.[36]

Ideally, the family, school, peers, and community all work in harmony. This provides a solid foundation of positive support and pro-social solid values. But when the ecology sends contradictory messages, children are in conflict. This is seen when teachers undermine family values, parents undercut teachers, or peers sabotage influence of the family. To understand a child, we identify supports and strains in the ecology.

Bronfenbrenner saw the *nature versus nurture* debates as meaningless since both biology and culture affect the brain and behavior. He called for detailed studies of children as biological beings living in the natural ecology of childhood – the family, school, peer group, and community. Bronfenbrenner also abandoned the *deficit* model of psychology in favor of focusing on strength and resilience. As children's bodies and brains mature, they continually face new challenges, thus the need for a developmental perspective.

While personal traits are important, behavior is always a *reciprocal transaction* with others, not a solo performance. A parent influences a child, but the child also influences the parent. The teacher impacts the student, but the student also has an effect on teacher behavior. Children select their peers and in turn are influenced by them. We live in reciprocity, joining together in a hymn of harmony or in a dance of disturbance.

Bronfenbrenner's bioecological model has strongly influenced world-wide policy and practice in every profession dealing with human development. He was instrumental in developing the Head Start program for children of poverty. He also had a life-long interest in troubled youth begun when his own father worked in a New York children's institution. He was closely tied to Nicholas Hobbs who pioneered ecological models for troubled and troubling children.[37] Finally the bioecological approach is breaking down barriers among the natural and social sciences, and building bridges between the stakeholders who must team together for positive youth development.

Deep Brain Learning

Education is what survives when what has been learned has been forgotten.[38]
- B. F. Skinner

Deep brain learning is a quest for lasting positive change and growth. Many youth today are concerned with looking good rather than doing good in the world. Our schools cannot challenge students to pursue *learning goals* to master life's challenges when we are obsessed with *performance goals* to raise test scores.[39] Behavior management systems that merely manipulate the surface behavior of youth will never build deep values and controls from within.[40]

How do we help young people wrestle with the big questions in their lives? The psychiatrists who authored *A General Theory of Love* offer this list of fundamental questions which merit our attention:

> What are feelings and why do we have them? What are relationships and why do they exist? What causes emotional pain and how can it be mended?… How should we configure our society to further emotional health? How should we raise our children and what should we teach them?[41]

Difficult problems are best solved by a consilience of perspectives. Thus, our discussion will be informed by fields as diverse as psychology, neuroscience, social biology, anthropology, sociology, psychiatry, pedagogy, and a rich tradition of values and practice expertise. One does not need to be an expert in any of these fields to tap the truths they offer. The following chapters draw together important findings on building healthy brains and positive interpersonal cultures so that young persons can successfully navigate pathways to resilience and responsibility.

[1] Key, 1909.

[2] Lloyd & Norfolk, 2007.

[3] Pestalozzi, 1801.

[4] Brühlmeier, 1976.

[5] Itard, 1801.

[6] Candland, 1995, p. 31.

[7] Lewis, Amini, & Lannon, 2000, p. 9.

[8] Lewis, Amini, & Lannon, 2000, p. 10.

[9] Lewis, Amini, & Lannon, 2000, p. 10.

[10] Lewis, Amini, & Lannon, 2000, p. 212.

[11] Lewis, Amini, & Lannon, 2000, p. 10.

[12] Carlsson-Paige & Lantieri, 2005.

[13] Skiba & Knesting, 2002.

[14] Krisberg, 2005.

[15] Heider, 1958.

[16] Morse, Cutler, & Fink, 1964.

[17] McDermott, 2004, p. 657.

[18] Anglin, 2002.

[19] Lakhoff, 2004.

[20] Anglin, 2002.

[21] Whewell, 1847.

[22] Wilson, 1998, p. 13.

[23] The origin of this saying is uncertain but it was popularized by Pope John Paul II during the period surrounding the millennium. Addressing the Pontifical Academy of Sciences in Rome, he contended that truths drawn from both science and religion are complementary.

[24] Jung-Beeman, 2008.

[25] Cooper, 2007.

[26] Mitchell, 2003.

[27] While random assignment to clinical trials may work in the clinic, it is ill matched to the real-world challenges of developing comprehensive interventions for youth. Kazdin & Weisz (2003) suggest various other research methods which provide useful evidence.

[28] American Psychological Association, 2006.

[29] van der Kolk, McFarlane, & Weisaeth, 2007, p. xi.

[30] Bronfenbrenner, 2005.

[31] Bronfenbrenner, 1977, p. 513.

[32] Bronfenbrenner, 2005.

[33] Phelan, 2004.

[34] Bronfenbrenner referred to the immediate environments of family, school, peers, and neighborhood as a child's microsystem. The interconnection of these environments is the mesosystem. Surrounding these spheres were increasingly broader circles of community influence called the exosystem and, finally, the cultural and societal forces of the macrosystem. In designing restorative interventions for individual children, the focus is usually on relationships in the microsystem and mesosystem which have more direct influence.

[35] Furstenberg et al., 1999.

[36] Lewis, 1997.

[37] Bronfenbrenner, 1984; Hobbs, 1982.

[38] Skinner, 1984, p. 484.

[39] Lewis, Amini, & Lannon, 2000, p. 13.

[40] Dweck, 1986.

[41] VanderVen, 2009.

CHAPTER ONE

Cultures of Discord

Our institutions are organized lovelessness.[1]
- Aldous Huxley -

STEVE CALLS HIMSELF A STORM TROOPER AND IS PART OF A SKINHEAD SUBCULTURE THAT REJECTS POSITIVE VALUES. *"I think it encourages mediocrity for the superior to help the inferior. The swift should not have to slow down for the lame. It encourages weakness…I got involved in Satanism, drugs, and every vile act possible in high school. Gee how many commandments can I break? I'm doing pretty good. I think I have only two or three left."*[2]

Modern society mass produces disconnected children. Throughout most of human history, the young were reared in close kinship communities. But today's nuclear family reduces social support to one or two biological parents. In response, many youth turn to peers to meet their primary needs for belonging.[3]

A century ago, sociologist Charles Cooley proposed that children form their self image by gauging the reactions of others who are important to them, which he called the *looking glass self*.[4] He warned that modern youth were becoming more beholden to peers than parents. From about age twelve, many come under the control of peer groups "in which their sympathy, ambition, and honor are engaged even more often than they are in the family."[5]

Many current theories of youth development see this shift of allegiance from parents to peers as normal and even a positive sign of maturity. In reality, it is an artifact of a society where there is a gulf between generations. In traditional cultures, children still grow to maturity immersed in relationships with elders. But today's typical adolescents spend only about 5% of their time with parents and 2% with other adults.[6] The remainder is spent with peers, on electronic media, or in isolation. The thinking, values, and identity of many modern youth are being shaped by the subculture of the immature.

The Absence of Elders

By nature, children and teens crave significant relationships with adults who care about them. Peers do not become the primary source of emotional support because this is normal but because adults are no longer key players in their world. According to Urie Bronfenbrenner, the excessive power of peers results when a "vacuum left by the withdrawal of parents and adults is filled with an undesired – and possibly undesirable – substitute of an age-segregated peer group."[7] Many contemporary youth are more preoccupied with pleasing their friends than making their parents proud. But peer groups aren't designed to provide the unconditional love and support of a caring family. When approval and acceptance are at the whim of peers, young people are only a step away from social abandonment. This makes modern teens intensely self-conscious and hyper alert to cues of rejection. Just hearing collective snickers from peers can cause sickening distress.[8]

Most youth are able to create something of a balance between loyalty to friends and to their family. But lousy outcomes are legion among children who have been betrayed by adults. Those who experience neglect, maltreatment, and emotional distancing from primary caregivers display deep shame and damaged self-worth.[9] Alienated and adult-wary youth gravitate to likeminded peers and hold adults at bay. However, the teen brain needs twenty years to mature and is not yet ready to operate solo from adult guidance.

Subcultures of adult-detached youth are hotbeds for problem behavior. Since teen brains crave novelty and excitement, risky activities have "benefits" of sorts, like having a blast at a wild party. Teens face exciting temptations at a time when their forebrain impulse control areas are not fully developed. But many youth operate in a secret world totally outside the influence of caring elders. Dramatic examples are countercultures of drugs and gangs, but the effect of the generational gulf is much more pervasive.

In earlier times, youth joined adults to build communities and explore the unknown wilderness. Today's teens troll the virtual wilderness of videogames and the world-wide web. Billions are spent on the digital simulation of deviance. Some of the most brilliant, violent videogames are produced by the military and distributed free to condition our children for combat.[10] The internet puts both educational and destructive information at youths' fingertips. Teens wander the web in search of wisdom to meet life's challenges. Those who are depressed can find websites offering support or explaining the best way to commit suicide. Computer chat rooms are devoid of normal social restraints. Anonymous internet conversations can quickly become sexual. Cyber bullying can escalate peer mistreatment to new levels of indignity. With all such problems, the question is not *what is wrong with today's youth?* but rather *where have all the elders gone?*

Don't Mess with Me!

Adults may condemn violence and in the same breath teach children to fight back. Many grow up in family or neighborhood cultures that sanction violence: it is not only appropriate but obligatory to attack those who have insulted you. If someone hits you – or even looks at you funny – you better hit him back.[11] To fail to fight back means you are weak and vulnerable.

> This attitude was evident in the recent television broadcast of a professional basketball game. After one or two fans threw something in their direction, basketball players who were leaving the basketball court entered the stands to engage in a brawl with the fans… they felt it was their right to avenge what they perceived to be disrespect to them.[12]

The core of this violence is a deeply embedded thinking error: *disrespect justifies aggression.* The person's private logic is expressed in beliefs such as these: *If I don't fight back, I will lose my respect. Never back down from a fight. Standing up will give me honor and respect. If I look weak, people will take advantage of me.*

In frontier areas of the United States, violence has long been acceptable to defend one's reputation. As late as the nineteenth century, Southern politicians shot one another in duels to avenge an insult. Social psychologists Nisbett and Cohen carefully document how this *Culture of Honor* was developed and perpetuated.[13] It might more aptly be called a *Culture of Revenge* since any disrespect justifies retribution.

Whether or not certain geographical regions have an affinity for violence traces back to the cultures from which colonists originally came. New England was first settled by farmers whose survival depended on a spirit of cooperation. In contrast, the South was first settled by Gaelic herdsmen who had to build reputations as furious fighters to protect their herds from being stolen. This herdsman mentality was also projected into the rangeland of the West. Similar folk theories of pre-emptive violence rule the mean streets: *If dissed, defend your reputation or you are in danger.*

Cultures of violence are perpetuated through child rearing practices. Violent adults model these reactions for children. But parents who coach kids to stand up and defend their rights may also inadvertently foster a culture of violence. They want their children to be tough and safe from harm. Instead, they create children who are thin-skinned and hyper-attuned to hostility. These young people are constantly at risk of being drawn into violence to protect their flawed definition of self-worth.[14] The results are conflicts in classrooms, macho violence on the streets, and thousands of young people expelled from school or incarcerated in the justice system.

The cultural belief that you never let anyone mess with you is deeply ingrained. While the original reason for vigilance against threat may have passed, the person still scopes the world in search of enemies. This superstitious belief now has gained a life of its own.[15] New provocations, however small, set off emergency alarms.

Persons hypersensitive to insult have highly threat-reactive brains. Laboratory studies show that they react almost reflexively to any insult as their brains spike wild levels of testosterone and stress chemicals. However, the problem is not brain pathology but personal and cultural experiences of violence that reprogram the brain.

Psychologists at the University of Michigan compared the emotional reactions of Southern and Northern males when treated with disrespect.[16] The subjects experienced a contrived insult, namely, being called *asshole!* by an actor employed by the experimenters. Southerners were often ready to go to the mat, reacting with anger. Saliva swabs showed that they also had a spike of testosterone and cortisol levels, signaling heightened stress and preparation to fight. Most Northerners thought the insulter was nuts rather than taking it personally.

Michigan researchers note that the culture of honor was exported from the South as cattlemen migrated to the Great Plains of the West. For example, Texan cowboys moved with their herds to South Dakota early in the twentieth century, importing their *don't mess with me* mindsets. They clashed with more peaceful farmers and, in the absence of Blacks, instituted cross-burning against Catholics and lynching of rustlers.[17] These habits of mind still persist in the region as seen in press accounts of abusive juvenile justice facilities and extremely high incarceration rates for juveniles.[18]

Dominance or Respect

Societies differ markedly in how they socialize power and aggression. Riane Eisler makes a distinction between cultures of dominance and partnership cultures.[19] Cultures of dominance operate under the principle of rule or be ruled. Partnership cultures create social order through values of mutual respect. By this standard, many so-called *primitive* cultures are more civilized and democratic than hyper-individualistic Western society.

At the deepest levels of emotion and belief, humans learn to approach others with mutual respect or in a contest for domination. While mothers are nurturers in all cultures, the role of the male varies greatly. The absence of the father in child rearing is associated with violent behavior among adolescent boys.[20] Cultures with attentive fathers also have much lower levels of violence.

Perhaps the most nurturing of cultures is the Aka tribe in central Africa where fathers spend nearly half of their day holding or within arm's reach of infants. Violence or corporal punishment is rare and, if one parent should hit an infant, this is just cause for the other parent to get a divorce. In Aka culture, the measure of a good man is being protective and affectionate to children. Yet in other societies, males see caring for children as a threat to masculinity. Thus, in a different African tribe, a man who carries a child in a sling would be harassed as being a homosexual.

In cultures of respect, males use their power and strength to protect. In cultures of dominance, this turns into aggression and subjugation of women and children and bullying of those who are seen as weak. These contrasting roles are alive and well in contemporary society. This was demonstrated by an intriguing study of machismo among young Mexican American males, mostly college students in the United States.[21] In Mexican culture, machismo has both positive and negative strains, Macho Dominance and Macho Respect.

Macho Dominance is marked by aggression, sexual domination, and hyper-masculinity associated with fights, substance abuse, and law breaking. Macho Respect[22] involves taking responsibility for protecting family and children and showing respect to all persons.

Since both models of masculinity are prevalent in most cultures, persons may incorporate aspects of each. However, these mindsets are radically different and show up as independent factors on statistical studies. Here are examples of key differences in the deep beliefs in these cultural mindsets:

Macho Dominance:
- Men are superior to women.
- Real men never let down their guard.
- It is necessary to fight when challenged.

Macho Respect:
- Men should respect their elders.
- Men must exhibit fairness in all situations.
- Men should be affectionate with their children.

The most striking difference was whether or not real men should be affectionate with children. Presumably such polarized beliefs reflect the individual's own childhood experience with males. A strong characteristic of Macho Dominance was alexithymia, the lack of attunement to one's feelings. Persons pursuing dominance do not reflect on their own emotions, nor are they empathetic with others.

Persons with Macho Dominance seek to rule women but are unlikely to gain real power in a group. They follow the core rule of bullying – victimize the weak – and thus do not make effective leaders. In contrast, Macho Respect enables one to exert influence on others through understanding and persuasion rather than raw power.

Dominance and respect reflect differences in brain function. Various lines of evidence suggest that toxic levels of testosterone are common in males who grow up in dangerous environments.[23] For example, boys without fathers may gravitate to gangs and become highly emotionally reactive, assuming others have violent intent.[24] Fear and aggression are contagious and can shape brain chemistry and behavior of all members of a social group.[25]

Hostility Toward Troubled Kids

Ironically, aggressive youth evoke hostile biases and labels from adults in their lives. Terms that come to mind include violent, antisocial, psychopathic, criminal thinking, predator, and more subtle pejorative terms used in formal diagnosis. Languages have thousands of words for personal characteristics or traits. Almost all of these are evaluative, either complimentary or derogatory. Whether applied to individuals or group members, they reflect respect and esteem or disrespect and dishonor.[26]

The use of threat labels for youth stirs strong negative emotions in adults who think like this. Any empathy is high-jacked by an amygdala reaction triggering the need to protect oneself. This "us against them" mindset dominates many correctional settings. It causes staff to believe that they must project images of threat to keep order and insure their own safety. This is shown

in the accompanying photograph from a Texas juvenile facility documented in the book, *No Place for Children.*[27]

Writing in the "kids are terrorists" genre is California psychologist-turned-crime-author Jonathan Kellerman.[28] He whipped out a little paperback for the popular press called *Savage Spawn*, fanning public fears of *violent* children. Kellerman never really worked with such kids, as his specialty as a young psychologist was children who were cancer victims. Never mind, he offers his opinion that children who are *antisocial* at eleven will likely become adult psychopaths. Some academic researchers peddle similar notions. Kentucky psychologist Donald Lynam launched a campaign to *import* theories about adult psychopaths for use in diagnosing childhood behavior problems.[29] He tars *fledgling psychopaths* with deficit-hyping descriptors:[30]

> The psychopathic individual is hot-headed, cold-hearted, impulsive, irresponsible, selfish, emotionally shallow, manipulative, lacking in empathy, anxiety, and remorse, and involved in a variety of criminal activities.[31]

Over a period of many years, the authors have worked directly with thousands of poorly socialized children who show weak conscience development. These are among the most vulnerable of our young. They desperately need to be reconnected to caring adults. When this happens, they are capable of dramatically turning their lives around.[32]

In practical terms, *zero tolerance* translates to disposing of kids, itself an act of violence. A Harvard civil rights project reported that over 3 million students were suspended and 87,000 expelled in a recent year.

In Chicago, public school expulsions increased over fifty fold in the first six years after these policies were adopted.[33] Furthermore, about 40% of suspensions are due to repeat offenders, which suggests the targeted students are not learning from this punishment. Past suspension is the best predictor of future suspension.

Corrective social experiences will be needed to reverse cultures and mindsets of violence. However, removal from school or placement in violent correctional settings only exacerbates the problem. Criminologist Lonnie Athens concludes:

> Banishing a student to the streets provides no solution to this problem but only displaces it to another part of the community where violence development will more likely be hastened than halted. Although belligerent students should not be permitted to disrupt instruction, school officials and teachers must look upon these students as needing special attention instead of ejection from their system.[34]

Professionals operating with a hostile bias about troubled youth will have little ability to understand these youth or connect with them. For sixty years, Bill Morse (1915-2008) trained professionals to work with challenging youth with this counsel: *if you don't recognize you might have ended up just like the most troubled young person you know, leave this work as your lack of empathy renders you useless.*[35]

An Awkward Fit

When our ecology fits our bio-social needs, humans flourish.[36] New Zealand psychiatrist Peter Gluckman's book *Mismatch* describes how modern culture no longer fits the design of our brains.[37] Our genes equip us to live in intimate kinship communities, not depersonalized masses. Humans can survive in a wide range of environments, but surviving is not the same as thriving. This mismatch causes physical disease, mental distress, and social disorder.[38]

Ecologies also vary in how well they can accommodate persons who are *different* or have unique needs. Temperamentally hyperactive boys may be heroes in cultures where males are hunters, but they are misfits in sedentary classrooms. Students who are headstrong and rebellious may be budding leaders but are at high risk in zero tolerance schools. While communities may be accepting of children with physical disabilities, those with emotional and behavioral impairments may be treated as outcasts.

In Australia, we encountered Helen Maczkowiack who had written the book *An Awkward Fit* to describe her son Stephen's desperate, lifelong struggle to belong. It was not until his suicide that she gained a window into his private world. On his computer was a chronicle of his attempts to find meaning in life, "to make all people and myself happy":

> I wish to be able to love without pain or loss.
> I would like to live without fear…
> I want a permanent friend…
> I wish there was a glimmer of hope that
> I could cheat death.
> I wish I had a reason to continue.[39]

As she pored over Stephen's private writings, she became aware for the first time that he had been struggling with Asperger's Syndrome, a high level autism that made it difficult for his brain to connect with the feelings of others.

Stephen failed to meet his most basic need to love and be loved. Such is the case of many modern youth. Gluckman notes that it is easier to change the environment than redesign the human brain. Thus our efforts need to be directed towards creating the ecologies for all children that are matched to their most basic nature.[40]

Tony: Growing Up in Prison

Tony Rios was brutalized as a small boy and developed a tough demeanor to protect himself. He had constant conflict in middle school and ended up on the street at age 14 where he was involved in a violent incident with an older homeless adult. Tried as an adult, Tony was sentenced to eight years in the South Dakota State Penitentiary. He spent much of his time locked in the hole *for behavior problems and never qualified for early release. Tony finally connected to the prison chaplain and a counselor from Reclaiming Youth. He finished his GED, completed his sentence, and returned to the community.*

I was just barely fifteen years of age when I walked in the prison to start an eight-year sentence for the crime of aggravated assault. I was sent to the minimum security prison because of my age. I was too young to qualify for any of the classes so I got a lot of minor write-ups because I had nothing to do. I was sent to the main prison where I was badly beaten because I refused to be strong-armed and bullied. My cousin was stabbed to death in this same prison. I began to miss my family and my mom, but they were too far away to console me. I was sent to the hole where I tried to take my life. I felt as if no one cared anymore so why not?

There was a riot in the prison and I became involved – it was better than having anyone pick on me. After the riot I was again placed in the hole and then in administrative segregation where I spent my 16th, 17th and 18th birthdays. I didn't care what I did or what happened to me. I had learned to shut all emotions off, so I wouldn't feel the pain of loneliness for my family. I was always depressed and suicidal and was constantly on psychiatric pills that dulled my thinking as well as my ability to hurt myself or others. I felt alone, confused, and depressed and the feeling of emptiness still haunts me.

At first, this place changed me into this unremorseful monster who would fight at the drop of a hat and didn't care about myself or anyone in general. It hardened me on the inside to a point that no one could get through to me with anything about where I was going in life. There was no one I could talk to who would listen with an open heart instead of an open book listing rules for prisoners. All I ever wanted was for someone to listen, someone who would understand what was going through my mind.

Building more prisons and juvenile facilities won't work as a deterrent to crime. The money should be used for better education and counseling for those youth who are falling into the wrong tracks in life. Prisons are a training ground for the young people who enter their cages. Once these kids graduate, they will commit more heinous crimes because they have received advanced psychological training in the criminal way of thinking.[41]

[1] Huxley, 1945, p. 96.

[2] Storm Trooper Steve, 1996, p. 127.

[3] Neufeld & Maté, 2005.

[4] Cooley (1902) called this the "looking glass self" to describe how our view of self is strongly influenced by how we think others see us. As will be discussed later, the brain actually has dedicated circuitry for the purpose of evaluating how we are seen in the eyes of others.

[5] Cooley, 1902, pp. 24-25.

[6] Csikszentmihalyi & Larson, 1984.

[7] Bronfenbrenner, 2005, p. 231.

[8] Packard, 2007.

[9] Sroufe et al., 2005.

[10] Lugo, 2006.

[11] Davis, 2006.

[12] Davis, 2006, p. 9.

[13] Nisbett & Cohen, 1996.

[14] Davis, 2006.

[15] Gordon Allport (1938) used the term "functional autonomy" to describe patterns of behavior that persist after their utility has passed.

[16] Nisbett & Cohen, 1996.

[17] Interviews March 2008 with Jim Ramey, Deadwood, South Dakota, age 92, former rancher and head of the South Dakota State Senate.

[18] A documentary of juveniles abused in correctional South Dakota boot camps and youth prisons was produced in 2001 by CBS: A three year nightmare. *Sixty Minutes II.* New York: CBS. January 2. Recent juvenile incarceration rates are three times the national average in South Dakota and Wyoming as reported by The Annie E. Casey Foundation in Kids Count 2008. www.aecf.org.

[19] Eisler, 1987.

[20] Hewlett, 1992.

[21] Arciniega, Anderson, Tovar-Blank, & Tracey, 2008.

[22] In Spanish this is called *Cabellerisomo.*

[23] Whether maltreated children become aggressive or retreat is related to variation in temperament and traits like anxiety or assertiveness.

[24] Gold & Osgood, 1992.

[25] Sapolsky, 2002.

[26] Nisbett & Cohen, 1996.

[27] Liss, 2005.

[28] Kellerman, 1999.

[29] Lynam, 1997, p. 425.

[30] This is based on pre-World War II studies of adult criminal traits by Georgia psychiatrist Hervey Cleckley (1941). Cleckley's term *mask* describes such persons as being highly skillful at concealing their real nature from those they exploit. In our experience, therapists who hold these deficit views will never be able to penetrate the *mask* put on by kids in pain in order to fend off those they do not trust.

[31] Lynam, 1998, p. 566.

[32] Seita, Mitchell, & Tobin, 1996; Brendtro, Ness, & Mitchell, 2005.

[33] Reinke & Walker, 2006.

[34] Athens, 1992, p. 95.

[35] Morse, 2008.

[36] Malinowski, 1960.

[37] Gluckman & Hanson, 2006. *Design* is a term used extensively in developmental biology but does not infer anything relative to discussions of intelligent design. Basically our body's design is shaped both by the genes we inherit and processes of development that bring us to maturity.

[38] Chomsky, 1979.

[39] Maczkowiack, 2006, p. 142.

[40] Gluckman & Hanson, 2006.

[41] Adapted from Rios, 1997, pp. 136-137.

CHAPTER TWO

Cultures of Respect

*Let us build communities and families in which our children
and youth, especially those who are most troubled, can belong.
Let us build a country in which our children and youth
can learn to care for and respect others.*[1]

- Nelson Mandela -

PHILIP IS A BRIGHT BOY WHOSE SEVERE CEREBRAL PALSY HAS KEPT HIM
FROM MAKING FRIENDS. *An intuitive math teacher, the school's wrestling coach,
encourages Philip to keep statistics during matches. Soon Philip is at every high
school game, keeping stats for all the sports. At the end of the year, during the
school's annual awards assembly, the athletes line the stage to receive their letters.
To Philip's surprise, the team captains call his name. As he makes his way slowly
down to the front, the school erupts into cheers. Philip beams with pride.*

Anthropologists who first studied children from Native tribes in
North and South America described them as radiantly happy, courageous, and
highly respectful of elders. Similar observations have been made about other
indigenous peoples worldwide.[2] However, only recently have truths from these
traditional systems of child development been seen as relevant to modern times.

Lakota psychologist Martin Brokenleg suggests that cultures which
deeply respect children share a strong commonality – they see children as
sacred.[3] The Lakota word for child literally translates as *sacred being*. The
Maori refer to a child as a *gift of God*. The descriptor for children in a Nigerian
tongue means *what wonders has God wrought!* The Zulu concept of children
evokes the feelings of joy they elicit in adults. Western culture strayed far
from the wisdom of the ages when it classified children as *chattel* along
with livestock and other possessions.[4]

15

Brokenleg and colleagues conceptualized the Circle of Courage, a consilient model of youth development integrating tribal knowledge, contemporary resilience research, and practice wisdom of youth work pioneers. Children in all cultures have four universal growth needs: Belonging, Mastery, Independence, and Generosity.[5] These are depicted in figures surrounding the four directions of a medicine wheel as drawn by Lakota artist George Blue Bird.

The Circle of Courage

generosity

independence

belonging

mastery

Rediscovering Lost Truths

How could supposedly "primitive" societies rear responsible children while modern civilization is plagued by conflict between generations? Sociologist Herbert Vilikazi from Zululand University suggests that the elders of tribal cultures have a more sophisticated knowledge of child psychology than the narrow perspectives of modern science.[6] The challenge for modern society according to Vilikazi is to rediscover these lost truths.

While all peoples are concerned with rearing healthy children, cultural practices are not always well-matched to this task. Mothers in Mayan tribes of Guatemala, like those in tribal cultures of India, are much more responsive to the needs of children than is common in Western child rearing. Small children in Polynesia watch others work and then pitch in to help as soon as they master simple skills.[7] In all of the world's traditional cultures, children grow to maturity immersed in interactions with adults and older peers as caregivers. Traditional kinship systems worldwide are designed so that children have many mothers, fathers, and grandparents.

In Western middle class society, children are intentionally segregated from the social world of adults. From toddler days, they are shunted off to age-graded schools. By adolescence, peer relationships take precedence over family and community ties.[8] Elsewhere in the world, most children's groups include a full range of ages, and children spend only about ten percent of their time with same-age peers.[9]

It was not until the nineteenth century that children in Euro-American culture were isolated by age group. This was seen as essential for efficiency in running factory schools. Today from earliest years, children are confined to artificial communities of the immature. This may serve adult convenience but does not meet the needs of children. Such arrangements seem normal to us but contradict the sweep of human history. Children are deprived of mature adult and peer models and of opportunities to relate with responsibility to their younger peers.

Harsh discipline is rare – and also quite unnecessary – in cultures where children and adults live in mutual respect. The attachment instinct motivates the child to emulate elders, not disobey them. In turn, the child's dependency activates the tending instinct in adults, rousing them to roles of protection and guidance. So it has been throughout the history of humanity. Such is the lost truth we must rediscover.

Rituals of Respect

From the moment I entered their village, I was captivated by their respectful behavior, self-confident demeanor, and astonishing creativity.[10] - Inge Bolin

Professionals who are told to build positive cultures or climates in schools and youth programs are often perplexed.[11] Even anthropologists who study cultures are not expected to create them. What might constitute the core of shared values in such a culture? In contemporary society, success is defined by wealth, power, and materialistic hedonism. The simple truth is that children are not always high on our personal priorities. And if a youth creates conflict in the community, strident voices call for punishment and exclusion.

Until recently, studies of youth development were limited to narrow views coming from middle class communities in Europe and North America.[12] For example, in the United Kingdom, it is an offense to leave a child under age 14 without adult supervision. But in many other communities worldwide, children begin taking responsibility for tending other children at half that age. Instead of playing with dolls, children become skilled caregivers for real babies.

Tribal cultures offer unique perspectives on positive youth development because they immerse children in *rituals of respect*.[13] Inge Bolin is a

 Canadian anthropologist who has lived with people from isolated mountain villages in highland Peru. While they are cut off from all of the supposed benefits of modern civilization, Bolin observes, "Children constantly amaze me in the manner in which they combine politeness and responsibility toward family and community with curiosity and surprising scholastic abilities."[14]

Respect for others is the most deeply ingrained value that guides all thought and action. Per the Circle of Courage resilience model, children from all cultures have needs for Belonging, Mastery, Independence, and Generosity. When these needs are met, children thrive. Many of the examples below are drawn from Bolin's study, *Growing up in a Culture of Respect.*

Belonging

Cultures differ dramatically in levels of nurturance for children. Northern European and American traditions sometimes resist the natural tendency of caregivers and children to bond. John Watson, the dean of American behavioral psychology, described mother love as "a dangerous instrument."[15] He proposed this arm-length approach to raising children in his famous 1928 book *Psychological Care of Infant and Child:*

> There is a sensible way of treating children. Treat them as though they were young adults…Never hug and kiss them, never let them sit in your lap. If you must, kiss them once on the forehead when they say goodnight. Shake hands with them in the morning. Give them a pat on the head if they have made an extraordinarily good job of a difficult task. Try it out. In a week's time, you will find out how easy it is to be perfectly objective with your child and at the same time kindly. You will be utterly ashamed of the mawkish sentimental way you have been handling it.[16]

In cultures of respect, child rearing is up-close and personal. Bolin offers this example of the intimate bonds between generations in the Quechua peasant community of Peru:

> Evenings are a time of fun, laughter, and storytelling. The girls sing and the boys and men sometimes play their instruments. Children are the center of attention before they retire to their sleeping corners. They are played with, joked with and tickled. They are never neglected, regardless of how tired parents and grandparents may be. Since loneliness is considered the saddest of states, everyone makes sure that no one lacks attention…at home and, if at all possible, in school, children are listened to and have the right to speak out for themselves.[17]

Attachment to adults is a prerequisite to learning from them. For millennia, the image of education was a group of children gathered around a respected elder. Children crave such guidance; and if they do not receive it from adults, they learn important life lessons by default from a gang of immature peers.

Mastery

While the desire to compete is universal, cultures shape its expression. There are two contrasting models: we either *compete with* or we *compete against* others. Typically in hierarchical cultures, the goal is to *fight hard* and to *beat* an opponent – note the combat metaphors. But many tribal cultures are horizontal rather than hierarchical. Thus when children of the Andes compete in activities or in school, they learn to give their best without setting themselves above others in roles of winners and losers.[18] Bolin explains that:

> …there is a difference between wanting to win to be better than others and using the "challenge" of others to give one's best. The former is a negative, aggressive approach to competition, and the latter is a positive, constructive, developmental approach… The satisfaction is not in winning but in seeing improvement in oneself over time.[19]

Children are taught not to flaunt their superiority. A wide range of physical and mental differences is accepted without prejudice and adolescents experience a low level of stress. Young people banter and joke continuously, but never does this escalate into insults or fights. Work well done is appreciated, but none are ever praised to the detriment of others. Nor do children brag of their achievements. As the talents of all are cultivated, all become winners.

Independence

Cultures of respect treat children as young citizens and responsible members of society. From age three, Quechua children begin doing all sorts of little jobs, like running errands and holding the bottle for a baby. They are proud to learn adult tasks and participate in ceremonies, eagerly joining in songs and dances. Adolescence is seen as a wonderful period of life as youth take on many of the rights and responsibilities of adults.[20]

The opposite of autonomy is coercion. Forcing a child to do something for which he or she is not ready is considered disrespectful.[21] This principle is embodied in the discipline practices of diverse tribal cultures. Lakota parents never used corporal punishment prior to the era of missionary and government boarding schools. The Semai tribe of Malaysia shares this philosophy:

> People do not often hit their children and almost never administer the kind of beating that is routine in some sectors of Euro-American society. A person should never hit a child because people say "how would you feel if it died?"[22]

In an egalitarian society with shared values of respect, there are models to follow but no one dominates or is subservient.[23] The core values of these traditional cultures are consistent with authentic principles of democracy. Cultures of respect do not demand blind obedience to authority. Instead, powerful bonds between the young and the old form the basis for discipline. Among Quechua children, autonomy is always balanced by a strong sense of responsibility toward others.

> I have never seen a small child being spanked, yelled at, or treated in a rough way. Yet children do not turn out to be spoiled. They soon learn about the behavioral norms that are accepted by family and community and demonstrated by adults and older siblings. At a young age they are introduced to the unwritten law of reciprocity, the hallmark of Andean life. This requires that respect be given and received in an eternal cycle that maintains their lives in balance.[24]

Generosity

Modern society deprives children of genuine opportunities to contribute to others. In contrast, cultures of respect immerse young people in service to the community. Adolescents are given apprenticeships and are always present at village meetings where processes of decision making are transparent. Cross-age positive networks provide opportunities to learn from those who are older and care for those who are younger. Youth are already using the skills of parenting and modeling values they have received from their elders. All children are expected to show concern and guide those who are younger, creating natural positive peer cultures.

Ancient ways of teaching respect are passed on to each new generation. Children participate in rituals, tending to their elders with food, drink, and courtesies. They care for younger children who in turn idolize them. They are challenged by meaningful activities that contribute to the community. As they approach adulthood, they join formal groups to help police their communities and solve social and community problems.

As children learn to show respect for others and all life, they are well on their way to being full contributing members of a community. Remarkably, the Quechua language has no word for respect. This is because respect is expected at all times. It is part of all thought and action and is never seen in isolation.[25]

Cultural Tails

In contemporary culture, many adults and youth are blatantly disrespectful – among peers and, even worse, towards one another. While adults quickly spot disrespect shown them by youth, disrespect toward children is so commonplace, we seldom even recognize it. Martin Brokenleg shares the following observation as seen through his anthropologically trained eyes:

A young upwardly mobile couple can be easily recognized by their clothing and trendy haircuts. Between them walks their child who is 4 or 5 years old. As they walk down the mall hallway, it is clear the child is tired and bored with all the shopping. Watching the parents speak is educational. The mother sometimes speaks to the child but just as often jerks on the lagging child's arm. At other times, she may direct the child's movement by pulling on an arm. It is obvious that the mother does not take the child's interests seriously. When the child wants to look in a shop window longer, the mother jerks him away. The child's requests to *look over there* are ignored or fully opposed.

One wonders if the mother uses these kinds of pulling and shoving with her work colleagues. If not, why does she use them on her own child? Is it because this child is hers as though he or she is some kind of property or possession? Perhaps the father is also disrespectful.

Farther down the mall, the father stoops down so his face is inches from his child's. In a too loud voice, the father shocks the child. "If you don't stop that whining, I'll give you something to cry about." The father's face is contorted with anger.

Does the man regularly use that tone of voice with his coworkers and friends? And if he does not, why does he use it with his own child? Perhaps the father's attitude is somewhat like the following: "This is only a child – not a human being and certainly not an adult or a real person. It isn't as though he or she has feelings or memory."

This may seem outlandish but it is not. The same kind of scene happens daily all across society, and what it shows is an inherited cultural devaluation of children, a devaluation that is such a part of Western society we don't even notice it. It is part of a deeply embedded practice, our *cultural tail* that we drag behind us, a thousand years long.[26]

Cliff: Balancing Two Worlds

Cliff Marshall, age 17, wrote about the challenges of growing up on the Hoopa Reservation in Northern California.[27]

Last year, in my Hoopa language class, a survey was taken asking the students why so many Native kids dropped out of school. One girl replied that the teachers did not understand that the Native kids have special needs. She was then asked what these special needs were but she could not answer in words the question she knew in her heart.

It is so much harder for Native kids to succeed because they are always forced to balance two worlds – the world that is theirs and the world of the dominant culture. No other children are ever faced with this obstacle.

Perhaps we are to blame for our own failure for, in this day and age, many of my Native people have become lost, disordered,…fickle. I do not mean to take away any pride from the people because we are very loving and strong in our beliefs, especially in loyalty to family, tradition, and religion. However, so many of us have fallen from grace – either to alcohol or drugs – that I believe the time for talking is over. The time has come for something to be done. I believe that to rebuild what we have lost begins with the youth.

The word for education literally means to *lead out*, but how – how do we do these things? How do we lead ourselves out? How do we emerge?

I believe that we as a people must rely on that which has been our greatest strength: our heart. Which brings me to a realization that I cannot fully put into words, for love cannot be taught. The most respected and beloved teachers I have known treated their students as their own family. Too many teachers today teach rubric and nothing else. They strive for high test scores, but do not connect with kids on a personal level, the kind of connection and respect that you show your own family.

Moreover, these kids need understanding and should not be reprimanded for something that is truly not their fault. For we are all born innocent. Is it their fault that they are born into a family of alcoholics or drug dealers? Is it their fault that their people are constantly angry because they survived near genocide? Most are born into poverty and hopelessness. How can they feel love, respect, and understanding when they have a school patrolled by police, with zero tolerance?

Since they have no true parental figures to guide them in making their decisions, they are forced to make decisions of their own. These children become adults at a young age. So adults must begin to treat them as somewhat of an equal. They must connect with youth on a personal level to help them make the right decision.

Teachers must observe students, as they each have a unique mind and way of thinking. They must help these kids through their life trials and be involved in their personal life. They can help youth who feel trapped overcome the circumstances they have been dealt. Let them know there are people who care. I know this is much to ask our teachers. But that is why you are our teachers. With your help, these kids may see the bigger picture. Then they can focus on a path of their own. I believe then we will find the answer.

[1] Mandela, 2003, p. 418.

[2] Rogoff, 2003.

[3] Brokenleg, 1998.

[4] Ariés, 1973.

[5] Brendtro, Brokenleg, & Van Bockern, 2002. The Circle of Courage has been applied world-wide in schools, treatment settings, and family and youth development programs. It provides the philosophical basis of the Reclaiming Youth movement. For more information on publications and training, see the Reclaiming Youth International website, www.reclaiming.com.

[6] Vilikazi, 1993.

[7] Martini & Kirkpatrick, 1992.

[8] Rogoff, 2003.

[9] Rogoff, 2003.

[10] Inge Bolin, 2006, p. 33.

[11] Cultures refer to the values, beliefs, and traditions of a particular community of individuals. Climate refers more narrowly to how persons experience that culture in their network of social relationships.

[12] Rogoff, 2003.

[13] Bolin, 1998.

[14] Bolin, 2006, p. xi.

[15] Watson, cited in Konner, 2002, p. 312.

[16] Watson, cited in Konner, 2002, p. 312.

[17] Bolin, 2006, p. 56.

[18] Bolin, 2006.

[19] Bolin, 2006, p. 154.

[20] Bolin, 2006.

[21] Bolin, 2006.

[22] Konner, 2002, p. 201.

[23] Bolin, 2006.

[24] Bolin, 2006, p. 152.

[25] Bolin, 2006, p. 160

[26] Brokenleg, Van Bockern, & Brendtro, 1999, pp. 2-3.

[27] Condensed from Marshall, 2004.

CHAPTER THREE

The Brain Terrain

*Without understanding the basic principles of how
the brain develops and changes, we cannot expect to design
and implement effective interventions.[1]*

- Bruce Perry -

PSYCHIATRIC DRUGS ARE BEING WIDELY PRESCRIBED TO CHILDREN
AND ADOLESCENTS. BUT MANY OF THESE YOUTH CRAVE OPPORTUNITIES
TO RESOLVE THEIR PROBLEMS INSTEAD OF MERELY RECEIVING
MEDICATIONS FOR THEIR DISTRESSED BRAINS.[2]

- *The therapist thought it was weird for me to cry so he gave me Prozac.
  But it didn't seem unnatural to me to feel sad after my mom left me.
  I didn't need meds. I needed my mother.*

- *I told my doctor I wanted to get off meds, and she just raised my meds.
  I told her I didn't want meds at all and she just changed my meds. I told her
  she was making me mad and she said, "We have pills for that."*

- *Medication is only a way of hiding pain and not allowing you to be yourself.*

The Brain Rules

Exciting research in neuroscience is deepening our understanding of children
and youth. Humans have specific brain programs which help us cope with
adversity, survive, and thrive. Blending this knowledge with findings from
resilience science provides a roadmap for prevention and intervention.[3]

"A brief glance into a modern textbook on neuro-physiology is all that
is needed to make one want to run and hide," says brain scientist John Ratey.[4]

But Einstein suggested that any scientific fact can be explained to any intelligent person if made as simple as possible but not simpler. This is the same way the brain creates order out of confusion: *keep it simple.*

In this chapter we highlight ten principles which we call *The Brain Rules*. Rules are *metaphors* since science uses *hypotheses* that are continually being questioned, not rules set in stone. *The Brain Rules* reflect these two ideas: 1) the brain is command central for all human behavior and 2) knowing how the brain operates can guide our work with children and youth. We begin our journey.

THE BRAIN RULES: 1

The human brain is the world's most complex system.

The brain has 100 billion neurons. Since the average human head has ten thousand hairs, all of the ten million people in New York City collectively have as many hairs on their heads as one human brain has neurons.[5] The brain communicates by electrical signals inside neurons and exchanges chemicals at the connection (synapse) between them. Each neuron has on the average 5,000 synapses and receives hundreds of signals from other neurons each millisecond.[6] If neurons were not enough, the brain has perhaps one trillion *glial (glue)* cells, named when it was thought their job was to hold the brain together. We now know that glial cells have important tasks including contributing the chemicals needed to form learning pathways. All of this is packed in a three-pound brain, which makes up 2% of the body mass yet uses 20% of the body's energy.

THE BRAIN RULES: 2

Learning involves connections in networks of neurons.

In 1895, Sigmund Freud, who was trained in neurology, proposed that neurons link together to create learning.[7] He described the synapse or space between neurons as a *contact barrier*. When two neurons fire together repeatedly, they form an association, the basis of all learning.

A half century later, Freud's principle was restated by Donald Hebb: *neurons that fire together wire together.*[8] The analogy of brains to computers was intriguing but turned out to be inaccurate. Computers are literally wired circuits sending electric signals at nearly the speed of light. Brains use electric impulses inside of each neuron but then have to portage chemicals across the gap between neurons. Typical brain signals travel one hundred miles an hour, although some poke along at a sleepy one mile an hour or speed up to 400 miles an hour in the super spindle neurons of our social brain.[9] A computer working this slowly would be junked.

More than a century after Freud proposed learning involves networks of neurons firing together, psychiatrist and neurobiologist Eric Kandel demonstrated this process. He showed that learning and memory result from strengthened connections between neurons. While short-term memory involves changes in synapses, long-term memory activates genes to grow new synaptic connections. For this work, he was awarded the 2000 Nobel Prize in Physiology and Medicine.

THE BRAIN RULES: 3

The brain makes meaning while computers only store data.

Natural human intelligence and mechanistic artificial intelligence are quite dissimilar. Humans are motivated to try to explain the unknown. We are literally driven to find some pattern in the chaos of life. The brain is engaged in a lifelong pursuit to make meaning of our world.[10]

Describing the brain with mechanistic wiring analogies is misleading. After decades trying to explain the brain as a computer, it is probably time to abandon these simplistic analogies. Computers are fast but dumb. Only the brain can change itself by constantly constructing new pathways, abandoning unused, dead-end trails, converting idle neurons from one task to another, and even creating millions of fresh brain cells from scratch. The brain not only learns, but it keeps looking for better ways to learn.[11]

Once we form a memory, the neurons know how to navigate these same pathways at a later time. How are they so smart? Whenever a network of neurons fires together, a *brain growth chemical* is produced so these neurons can locate the same pathway at a future time.[12] This chemical also stimulates growth of insulation (myelin) around the individual neuron axons so they become 100 times more efficient than before. Experience creates enduring connections following pathways across millions of neurons.

The lower survival brain is the first region to develop.

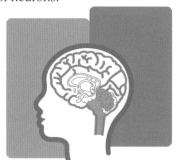

One of the most useful ideas about how the brain works is the concept of the triune brain, put forth by neuroscientist Paul MacLean.[13] We get three brains for the price of one, and each sub-brain has a unique task. To simplify, these are the primary tasks of the triune brain: the lower survival brain *reacts*, the deep emotional brain *values*, and the higher logical brain *reasons*.[14] These three brains are interconnected so they can work in unison, but sometimes they clash.

The lower survival brain shown in the accompanying figure is first to develop in the growing fetus. It keeps our body in balance by controlling autonomic functions like heartbeat and respiration. This brain stem is perched atop the spinal cord and contains pathways to execute motor behavior. If danger is detected, the survival brain activates fight and flight reactions, switching the brain into overdrive to deal with threat.[15] All of the activities of this lower brain are automatic and reflexive. In cases of extreme panic, this lower brain overrides thought and reason. With growing maturity, it can be regulated to some extent by higher brain areas.

*The deep emotional brain is the center
for motivation.*

The emotional brain is shown in the
accompanying figure. *Emotion* and *motivation*
come from the same root word meaning *to
move*. Emotions motivate action. We like to
think of ourselves as logical beings, but the
emotional brain is in charge of much more

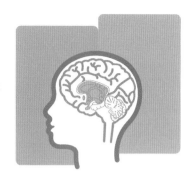

than we might have imagined.[16] It tells us what is worth remembering.[17]
The brain would be flooded and overwhelmed if there was not some method
for prioritizing. The brain uses *novelty* as the strategy for focusing our attention.[18]
We need a signal to say, *pay attention, this may be important to remember.*

The sentry of the emotional brain is the *amygdala* which is shown in
the figure below. Its name is the Greek word for almond. We have two of these
almond-shaped structures inward from the temples.
The amygdala spots incoming stimuli as pleasurable
or threatening, registering any variation from normal
as a potential danger or opportunity. Of particular
interest is that the amygdala reads tone of voice
and facial expressions to separate friend from foe.
Any stimuli that is novel or threatening is noticed by the
amygdala which then mobilizes the appropriate emotion.

The amygdala connects to the *hippocampus* which is the memory
switchboard. The hippocampus (Greek for seahorse, signifying its shape)
registers emotionally charged events, stores them for a time, and then files
permanent memories elsewhere in the brain for later retrieval.

Emotions are not *primitive* but sophisticated deep brain intelligence.
Lacking this emotional compass, the logical brain would run in circles,
unable to make decisions or take action. Emotions enable us to deal with
important life events without stopping to plan out a logical sequence of action.[19]

The higher logical brain is the center for reasoning.

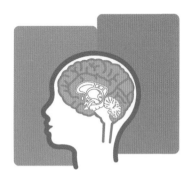

This is the last brain area to mature. Pictured in the accompanying figure, this is sometimes called the *cortex* (bark) because it wraps around the deeper brain areas. It is distinguished by many wrinkles and folds that create more surface area for learning and memory. This cortex is much more developed in humans than in other animals in order to manage our sophisticated systems of culture and social relationships.

The word *logic* has a broader meaning than conscious reasoning. The higher brain has the capacity for several kinds of logic:

- perceptual motor logic (rear brain areas)
- verbal analytic logic (usually handled by the left brain)
- emotional logic (mostly processed in the right brain)
- intuitive logic (develops in the frontal brain areas)

The Orchestra Conductor: A Job Description

The frontal area of the higher brain plays a role like that of an orchestra conductor.[21] It monitors messages from all other brain areas and enables persons to respond intelligently. In contrast, immature brains and those of lower animals are mainly reactive. Daniel Siegel provides this job description for the orchestra leader:

1. Regulate bodily state by taking charge of fight and flight reactions.

2. Manage emotions to respond purposely instead of reacting impulsively.

3. Attune to others with empathy to understand their feelings and thoughts.

4. Gain insight into one's self using stories of life events.

5. Notice signals from bad "gut feelings" and good "heartfelt feelings."

6. Develop a morality of right and good and act on pro-social values.

7. Make wise decisions to meet one's needs and insure well-being.

The logical brain matures slowly, beginning in the rear sensory-motor areas. Language and social areas develop profusely throughout childhood. Last to mature is the frontal cortex that handles *executive functions*.[20] It serves as an orchestra conductor to keep all brain functions in harmony. This includes managing emotions, planning ahead, and making wise decisions. While survival and emotional brain capacities operate from birth, the logical brain takes more than twenty years of cultural experience to mature.

The right and left brain specialize in different tasks.

The logical brain is split into right and left hemispheres.[22] In 95% of humans, the left brain handles speech and language.[23] While the left brain specializes in logical analysis, the right brain adds more global information including nonverbal and emotional cues.

When aroused, the left brain tries to solve problems by coming up with *logical* theories and explanations. Even if no cause is obvious, the left brain is compelled to invent reasons and make up a story.[24] For example, eight-year-old Melanie learns the terrible news that her parents are divorcing so she decides it must be her fault because she was bad.

Encountering a stressful event, the right brain checks this out against its storehouse of emotional memories to see how to react to this problem. Since the right brain is closely tied to the amygdala, it is more fear based. It reads facial expressions and tone of voice and activates anxiety and avoidance behaviors. This region registers distress from rejection or social exclusion. Such emotions lead us to retreat – or to attach to a trusted person for safety and reassurance.[25]

In general, the right brain deals with fear, anxiety and depression while the left brain handles happiness.[26] Positive emotions direct us to explore the environment, approach others, and stay involved. The left brain initiates approach behaviors including friendly extraversion but also some acts of purposeful aggression.[27]

In highly stressful situations, the right brain exercises veto power over the left. The resulting anxiety, fear, or trauma memories override positive emotions and leave us speechless.[28] The main resource for managing trauma and negative emotions is the verbal brain. By sharing and reflecting on experiences in a safe and trusting relationship, we are often able to calm turbulent emotions.

THE BRAIN RULES: 8

Various memory systems are used for different purposes.

I sometimes wish I could start my life over not knowing anybody because I have almost no good memories. When I was four, I was with my Dad when he shot himself. I have always tried to figure out what I did wrong, why he didn't want to keep being my Dad.[29] - Jonathan

Our brains have separate areas for short-term and long-term memories. We also are able to draw from both conscious *(explicit)* and unconscious *(implicit)* memory. Our private logic about ourselves and the world is heavily determined by our autobiographical memory which includes important life events.[30]

Short-term memory is like working on temporary images pulled up on a computer screen. They are fleeting and do not make permanent changes in brain pathways. We only can concentrate on a limited number of words or ideas without overloading short-term memory. For example, most people can remember only about seven numbers in a sequence. For this reason, short, succinct, verbal phrases are easier for the brain to understand. And if we want ideas to transfer from short-term to long-term memory, we need to keep them simple and potent. An example is seen in advertising jingles.

Long-term memories are like permanent files in deep storage. These memories are laid down in various regions that archive words, images, and actions. The amygdala stores our conditioned emotional reactions to these events, and the hippocampus indexes these memories for later recall.

Significant life events are stored in autobiographical memory. These are recovered as narratives by the storyteller in each of us. In general, episodes that cause great pleasure or pain are most likely to be recalled. Traumatic events are the most troubling since these negative experiences from the past continue to pop up and intrude on current activity.

Our brains are specifically designed to keep remembering uncompleted tasks, which is called the Zeigarnik Effect. For example, if you have trouble recalling the name of a person immediately, it is likely to pop up a short time later. The brain is doing what it does best, finding answers to unsolved problems.[31]

Half the cells in the higher brain are connected with vision, so it is not surprising that visual memories are the most enduring. Likewise, the most potent words are those that evoke visual images.[32] When children have difficulty understanding or remembering concepts, it is often helpful to convert these into pictures.[33]

"You never forget how to ride a bike. People don't forget any capacity that depends on feel rather than fact."[34] The deep brain is a massive storage center for key life experiences. When we repeatedly practice certain procedures, like riding a bike, these become automatic. Such memories are stored as entire patterns of behavior which can be executed without conscious planning.

The brain stockpiles a lifetime of experiences which vastly exceed what can be readily recalled in conscious memory. Repeated experiences engrave brain pathways which shape our thinking, values, and behavior. Thus, being reared with rituals of respect – or disrespect – creates deep brain learning.

THE BRAIN RULES: 9
The brain rules but Nature and Nurture share the throne.

Debates about nature versus nurture pose a false dichotomy. The two are so intertwined that it would be like arguing whether a goose flies because of wing genetics or air currents. The human brain is the prize handiwork of the human genome. Perhaps two-thirds of its genes are involved in building and operating the brain. But the most remarkable new insight is that experience plays a central role in turning these genes on or off. Genes shape experience but experience also shapes genes.[35]

34

Many childhood problems trace to common variations in biological temperament which anthropologist Ruth Benedict called *cradle traits*.[36] Whether these traits are seen as normal or deviant varies from one society to another. Likewise, children in the same family who have different temperaments will draw out different reactions from caregivers.

Since the nineteenth century, scientists have known that genes can shape behavior. What is remarkable is the discovery that experience can activate genes to grow new neurons. This calls for linking together bodies of knowledge about brain and culture that heretofore have been separated.[37] Children face a double risk from unhealthy environments which impact both their behavior and their brains. Adults are responsible for creating cultures where young brains can thrive.

THE BRAIN RULES: 10

Our brains are resilient and able to adapt to new challenges.

One of the most exciting new developments in brain science is research on *neuroplasticity*. *Neuro* refers to brain cells, and *plastic* means malleable. Neuroplasticity is the ability of the brain to lay down new pathways. We now know that the brain has remarkable powers to change its own structure and compensate for even the most challenging biological and social risks.[38]

Early brain development is important because it builds a foundation for subsequent growth. However, there is much misinformation suggesting that lack of proper early stimulation creates irreversible problems. In a wide variety of cases, plasticity allows the brain to rewire itself. Although, traumatic experiences may alter the brain's structure as seen on a scan, this image only captures the brain at a moment in time and does not show what it is capable of becoming.[39]

Plasticity in children entails periods of exuberant brain growth followed by pruning of neurons. One study suggests that these growth spurts are likely to occur at 2, 4, 7, 11, 15, and 19 years of age, coinciding with changes in cognitive development.[40] Whatever the exact times of surges might be, it

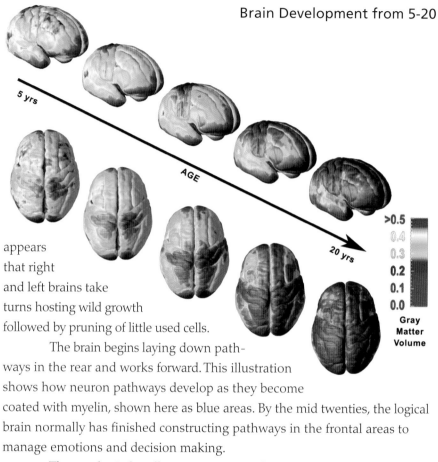

5 yrs

AGE

20 yrs

>0.5
0.4
0.3
0.2
0.1
0.0

Gray
Matter
Volume

appears
that right
and left brains take
turns hosting wild growth
followed by pruning of little used cells.

The brain begins laying down path-
ways in the rear and works forward. This illustration
shows how neuron pathways develop as they become
coated with myelin, shown here as blue areas. By the mid twenties, the logical
brain normally has finished constructing pathways in the frontal areas to
manage emotions and decision making.

The rear brain handles sensory-motor functions and young children
are live-wires of exploration and activity. Language areas in midbrain also
come on-line early. By preadolescence, brain development starts shifting to
more frontal areas. With children showing signs of ADHD, this process is often
delayed. They continue to operate in their sensory-motor areas for three to
five more years but eventually follow the normal pattern of development.[41]

The young brain has remarkable plasticity and can redesign itself.
If children have not learned to master certain life challenges at one develop-

mental stage, they get more opportunities through the on-going redesign of the brain. Time is an ally in developing new brain circuits for self-regulation. Neuroplasticity is the brain's equivalent to resilience, adapting to cope with challenge.

Humans need highly resilient brains because our learning is life long. The adult who does not continue to grow and change becomes stagnant. Muhammad Ali once said, "The man who views the world at 50 the same way he did at 20 has wasted 30 years of his life."[42] Wise elders become the repositories of cultural wisdom in their later years. Many older brains are uniquely adept at story telling as they retrieve a rich trove of experience and cultural values which they convey to the young.

The Vital Balance

As we have seen, various areas of the brain work together to meet challenges and keep our biological and psychological balance. Antonio Damasio uses a tree to demonstrate the brain mechanisms that keep bodily and mental functions in a state of homeostasis.[43]

The levels of the tree depict various levels of brain function. Near the trunk are the automatic brain stem reflexes and regulatory systems. Next come areas that alert us to our external environment by pain and pleasure signals tied to approach or avoidance reactions. In the middle branches are deep systems designed to meet survival and safety needs as well as developmental needs, including attachment, achievement, autonomy, and altruism. Primary emotions such as fear, anger, sadness, surprise, and revulsion are present in many animals as well as humans. Next come the social emotions such as empathy, embarrassment, shame, guilt, pride, jealousy, envy, gratitude, admiration, indignation, and contempt. Social emotions are tied both to the thinking brain and to deep emotional centers. Finally, our conscious mind becomes aware of these states through feelings which are processed in our thinking brain.[44]

In his classic book, *The Vital Balance*, psychiatrist Karl Menninger (1893-1990) notes that early diagnostic systems merely slapped labels on whatever one did not understand very well.[45] But science is now discovering how various biological and cultural factors combine to create disequilibrium and how the human brain and personality seek to achieve a "vital balance." This important idea was expressed by Spanish Muslim scholar Ali ibn Hazm (994-1064):

> No one is moved to act, or resolves to speak a single word, who does not hope by means of this action or word to release anxiety from his spirit.[46]

Ryan: Stressing to the Max

Ryan, a sixteen-year-old student from Australia describes his turbulent family and school life and distrust of professionals who chose to medicate instead of understand.

I was getting good grades till my mum's boyfriend moved in and started beating us. That's when I started having problems. Then the school started complaining about my lack of motivation and attendance and my behavior. I was stressing to the max. I would be sitting in class trying to concentrate but can't. Too many things running through my head. I can't shut my mum out of my head. I'd be sitting there with all these thoughts. They just don't go away.

Then I'd struggle with my anger. I became really pissed off easily, I would tell the teacher to f--- off and end up in the principal's office. Then you know at the psychologist's office, doing some dicky anger program. It's like get fucked, you don't even know nothing. Then they sent me to this psych for some assessment and he told me mum that I was ADD. So they put me on this medication, Dexies (Dexamphetamine), to settle me. They didn't know what they were talking about and when it didn't work, they upped me medication. Being told I was having a disorder, like the mental problems are all my fault. That psychologist should spend a night with my step-father, see if he can sort that fuckwit out so me mum would be safe. See how he'd handle getting smashed every night.

Me go to counseling? What for?! They'd probably diagnose me with something else. What do these people know about me and what I think and go through? They don't see what goes on outside their comfy office. I could teach them a thing or two. You feel that they sort of look down on you. You feel pissed at them cause they don't understand and then want to tell you what you should do with your life.[47]

[1] Perry & Hambrick, 2008, p. xx.

[2] California Council on Youth Relations, 2007, pp. 17-18.

[3] Brendtro & Longhurst, 2006.

[4] Ratey, 2002, p. 9.

[5] Sylwester, 2005.

[6] Wexler, 2006.

[7] Freud, 1895/1954.

[8] Hebb, 1949.

[9] Doidge, 2007.

[10] Brown, 1991.

[11] Doidge, 2007.

[12] The technical term for the brain growth chemical is Brain Derived Neurotrophic Factor or BDNF for short.

[13] MacLean, 1990.

[14] Goleman (2006) follows LeDoux in using the words "high road" and "low road" to refer to logic and emotion. The semantics imply that emotions are primitive and logic is refined. This fits a strong bias in academic circles but it does not hold up to science. Thus, we will use three shorthand terms to refer to triune brain functions: higher brain (logic), deep brain (emotion), and lower brain (survival). These visual images are easy to grasp, and better match neuroscience.

[15] Johnson, 2004.

[16] Bath, 2005.

[17] The emotional brain is sometimes called the limbic system because it wraps around the survival brain like a girdle (limbus in Greek).

[18] Berns, Cohen, & Mintun, 1994.

[19] Ekman, 2003.

[20] Goldberg, 2001.

[21] Siegel, 2006.

[22] The emotional brain is also divided into two hemispheres. Thus, we have an amygdala and hippocampus in both the left and right hemispheres.

[23] Brocha's area near the left temple is believed to have first specialized in sign language and subsequently in spoken language.

[24] Gazzaniga, 2008.

[25] Cozolino, 2006.

[26] Ratey, 2002.

[27] Harmon-Jones, 2007.

[28] Lupien, 2004.

[29] Condensed from Lay, 2000.

[30] Foer & Steber, 2007.

[31] Zeigarnik, 1927.

[32] Cozolino, 2006.

[33] Grandin, 1995. Growing up with autism, Temple Grandin taught herself to convert abstract ideas into pictures as a way to understand them.

[34] Lewis, Amini, & Lannon, pp. 113-114.

[35] Huttenlocher, 2002.

[36] Benedict, 1959, p. 278.

[37] Wexler, 2006.

[38] Doidge, 2007.

[39] Grafton et al., 2006/2007.

[40] Dawson & Fischer, 1994.

[41] NIH, 2007. An organization established by Thomas Szaz proposes an alternate hypothesis, i.e., that the delay in development may be related to medications given to these children. www.cchr.org.

[42] Cozolino, 2006, p. 46.

[43] Damasio, 2003.

[44] Damasio, 2003.

[45] Menninger, 1963.

[46] Hazm, circa 1064, cited in Menninger, 1963, pp. 83-84.

[47] Excerpted from Glasson-Walls, 2004.

Trust Maps

To be included in relationships in which one feels known,
heard, seen, and understood is a biological necessity.[1]

- Kalman Glantz & John Pearce -

AFTER A FEW WEEKS IN HIS NEW ALTERNATIVE SCHOOL, 14-YEAR-OLD
DAVID IS WARY. *Why are the other kids acting so interested in him? What are
they after? Where he comes from, there's no such thing as friendly. If somebody
starts getting too close, it isn't about friendliness. It's about finding vulnerability.
This is different somehow. Everybody talks upfront to everybody.*

Learning is not just neurons chasing blind trails through the cerebral
woods. Instead, the human brain uses inbuilt maps to help us learn what is
most important for survival. For example, children naturally learn to fear spiders
but not butterflies. The child's brain is also primed to fear strangers but to
hunger for familiar human faces. Researchers call these brain programs
"prepared learning."

Global positioning devices have built-in maps to guide one to a
destination. Our brains also come equipped with maps to meet challenges
common to all humans.[2] To thrive, young people need to build relationships,
explore their world, gain self-control, and contribute to others. The following
chapters will highlight how the brain prepares us for this learning through
inbuilt maps for trust, challenge, power, and moral development.

Trust

The slightest mistrust, the smallest unkindness, the least act of injustice or contemptuous ridicule, leave wounds that last for life in the finely strung soul of the child. While on the other side unexpected friendliness, kind advances, just indignation, make quite as deep an impression.[3] - Ellen Key, 1909

The need for trusting relationships is as basic a need as hunger or thirst.[4] The first study of human bonding was conducted in the 13th century by Holy Roman Emperor King Frederick II. The king spoke several languages and hoped to discover the natural inborn language by raising children who would never hear speech. He hired nurses to suckle and bathe children, but they were forbidden to speak to them. His experiment ended in disaster as all of the children died before uttering a single word. The King concluded that "children could not live without clapping of the hands and gestures and gladness of countenance and blandishments."[5]

Across all cultures, humans bond together for social support. They prefer to spend much of their time in groups, invest in socializing children, and draw on support from elders. Children develop strong attachments to their primary caregivers and rejection always has a malignant effect on development.[6]

The human social brain is the secret of our survival on this planet. We are not physically endowed to compete in the animal kingdom. We lack sharp teeth or claws; we cannot outrun predators, fly away, or hide under water. Instead, our survival depends on living in supportive groups. When under threat, we band together to befriend and protect each other.[7]

From birth, the brains of children are prepared to focus on human faces. "These small areas of skin are the most scrutinized area of the planet."[8] The face is the primary display board for human emotions.

> Science has discovered emotionality's deeper purpose: the timeworn mechanisms of emotion allow two human beings to receive the contents of each other's minds. Emotion is the messenger of love; it is the vehicle that carries every signal from one brimming heart

to another. For human beings, feeling deeply is synonymous with being alive.[9]

The amygdala instantly detects cues of safety or threat through eye contact, facial expressions, gestures, and tone of voice. Children's survival is dependent on adults and so they continually search for evidence that they are valued. "All I want is some kind of noticement," said Daniel, a troubled boy in a Cleveland alternative school.[10]

Erik Erikson explained that a child yearns "to be gazed upon by the primal parent and to respond to the gaze, to look up to the parental countenance and to be responded to."[11] Children want someone to admire who returns their affection and gives them support. They first find this guiding light and acceptance in parents and family, then in peers and companions. Even as adults, we search for some *numinous*, a source of inspiration beyond ourselves.

The need for belonging permeates all of our relationships. It begins with bonds between children and caregivers and extends to friendships, sexual bonds, and helping behavior.[12] These patterns are universal across cultures since they are designed into our DNA.

Human attachment is closely intertwined with the need for safety.[13] Attachment involves proximity, and humans feel safest in the presence of trusted persons. Children run to their parents' bedroom in the middle of the night when frightened by a thunderstorm or a bad dream. Neuroscience tells us they are rushing for a dose of oxytocin.

Oxytocin and Trust

Oxytocin is the hormone for social bonding.[14] It is central to parental, fraternal, sexual, and benevolent relationships.[15] While cortisol is the primary stress hormone that revs up the brain, oxytocin creates trust and calms the brain.[16] Secure, trusting relationships regulate emotion and turn off the stress response.[17]

Other hormones combine with oxytocin in various kinds of relationships involving attraction, attachment, empathy, or lust. Human bonds are

44

maintained over the long haul by these very pleasurable chemicals in the brain. Love is a many splendored chemical thing.

Oxytocin makes better partners and parents – in both people and prairie dogs. Only three per cent of all mammals form lasting pair bonds. Prairie voles mate for life and both males and females participate in parental care. The reason appears to be that both genders have a rich supply of oxytocin. A relative of the prairie vole is the montane vole, which looks remarkably similar but is oxytocin deficient. These males are promiscuous and ignore their young.[18] Without oxytocin, the animals are fickle partners and deadbeat dads.

In general, females have more oxytocin than males, and males have more vasopressin, which also contributes to social bonding. Both of these closely related chemicals are crucial in tending behavior and loyalty to partners and kin.[19]

Oxytocin helps us let down our guard and trust others. It is released during positive social interactions and permits expression of vulnerable behaviors. Oxytocin also can calm aggression associated with testosterone.

Vasopressin makes us courageous protectors of those we love. It plays a role in vigilance and guarding of mate and offspring, a behavior seen in both sexes but more often associated with males.[20]

The hormones associated with trust are antidotes to all painful emotions. Rejection and abandonment plunge us into fear, anxiety, and shame. Trust turns off the amygdala alarm and frees us from this pain. "Learning anything positive, including love, requires freedom from fear."[21]

Caregivers calm emotions until children learn to do this solo. Until their higher brain controls are operative, children must borrow the prefrontal cortex of the adults as a model for their own developing brain. Each time we help children move from agitation to a calm and regulated state, they build pathways for self-control. Ideally, this happens early in life, but for many children, this is the goal of teaching and treatment.[22]

The Social Brain

Curiosity is the brain's most pervasive human emotion, and prime brain pathways are dedicated to social curiosity.[23] Humans have profound social interests; while we can discuss any topic imaginable, we mostly talk about people. Daniel Goleman suggests that social intelligence is not just a sideshow in the thinking brain. In fact, general intelligence is an offshoot of social intelligence.[24] The brain's primary design is to negotiate our social world. In many cultures, *intelligence* is not academic proficiency but interpersonal prowess. Recent research on *mirror neurons* and *spindle neurons* shows how much of the brain is designed to meet social challenges.

Elaborate networks of mirror neurons in the human brain insure that every generation of children will imitate the behavior of their caregivers. Mirror neurons enable children to effortlessly acquire one or more languages without formal instruction. (By the teen years, one has to use other brain areas so language learning becomes more tedious). Mirror neurons enable us to acquire elaborate social skills just by observation. When the mirror neurons do not operate correctly – as in autism – children experience a host of developmental impairments.

Rizzolatti, who discovered mirror neurons, explained that this brain ability helps us understand the minds of others, not through logical reasoning but by becoming attuned to their brains.[25] Young children are highly attentive to their caregiver's emotions and behavior. Only hours after birth, infants start mirroring adults. Mirror neurons permit them to adjust their turbulent emotions to the mother's calm state. As they mature,

mirror programs enable children in a group to attune to social behavior of one another.[26] Mirror neurons explain why crowd behavior becomes contagious and how we get caught in conflict cycles. And, mirroring can be fun; even adults enjoy group activities where all act in unison, whether in the cheers of a crowd at a sports event or in the singing of a choral group.

Spindle neurons are the switchboard of the social brain.[27] The fastest neural circuits, they track our interpersonal interactions and guide snap social decisions. Whenever we are not distracted by other tasks, we log on to this "relationship hotline." The spindle neurons are located directly behind the eyes and connect throughout the brain, but particularly to our emotional centers. Spindle cells start developing after birth and are dependent on social experience. Early neglect and trauma can delay development of these neurons.

Children continually scan their social world to determine what others think of them.[28] Adults are also very hyper-alert to being watched. In one experiment, employees were placed on the honor system to put money for their refreshment breaks in a cash box. This depository for donut money was placed beneath a prominent picture – which alternated weekly between flowers and a pair of watchful eyes. Cash contributed was 2.76 times more when eyes were looking down at the employees.[29] Our brain reacts powerfully to faces and eye contact, even in pictures.

In traditional cultures, children are under the *watchful eye* of adult and peer caregivers. From the first year of life, the child is able to detect where the eyes of others are directed. The sense of being watched is a primary behavior control at any age. Parenting language is rich with references like *keep an eye on the kids* or *don't let them out of your sight*. Religious writings also describe the Deity as *watching over* humans. In the words of a familiar hymn: "His eye is on the sparrow, so I know He's watching me." But in elder deficient cultures, few eyes are on children and almost none on teens.

Bids to Connect

Humans use specific behaviors to make *bids* for connection. Eye contact, smiling, laughter, and touch are all deep-brain bonding signals. These release oxytocin and create strong feelings of attraction and well-being. Oxytocin has a short half life and is gone in minutes, but the joy of these small signs of affection can bond persons to one another, even during times of trial.

Physical touch can be a powerful means of providing support and soothing stress.[30] Of course, such contact makes one vulnerable so it is only effective when trust is secure. Human touch connects to the core of the social brain and conveys emotional warmth. There are great cultural differences in how much human touch is encouraged or inhibited. The many restrictions on touch in schools and treatment programs can work against creating trusting communities. Contact with pets can create some of the same effects by activating the affiliative centers in the brain.[31]

Laughter also stimulates social bonding. It signals positive intentions and conveys that one is accepted and part of a group. Humans have a brain-based laugh detector which in turn activates our laughter generator.[32] Children laugh and smile more than adults, probably because their brains are more focused on recruiting relationships.

Emotions of delight spring from the lower areas of the brain that regulate approach or avoidance.[33] A spontaneous deep brain laugh is unlike a forced laugh which is only a superficial motor behavior. Social survival requires spotting the difference between genuine laughter and smiles and contrived versions.[34] Even children can tell authentic enjoyment from polite or false friendliness.

Swedish brain scientist Bjorn Merker studied children who had a rare condition of being born without a cortex.[35] Some of the parents had been told by neurologists that their child had a brain *like that of a reptile* and would be vegetative. But when reared in loving families, such children laugh and smile in the uniquely human manner. At the deepest levels, our trust maps are formatted for friendliness.

The human brain is so tied to the rewards of social contact that persons who are disconnected feel great emptiness. Even their immune systems are compromised. In effect, our brains are oxytocin addicted to bonds of trust.

Ironically, drugs of abuse can mimic this natural high of human bonding. This is why social exclusion is so counterproductive, it weakens social bonds. Likewise, some psychoactive drugs prescribed to manage behavior have the effect of lowering oxytocin levels which may impede relationships and therapeutic alliances.[36] Substance abuse is often an attempt to compensate for the biochemical rush of positive relationships.

Lacking the chemistry of love, many pursue the love of chemicals. Addicts may satisfy their need for intimacy by manipulating the biochemistry of bonding and attachment. Cocaine, ecstasy, and some other drugs are thought to achieve at least some of the effects of the brain that relationships would otherwise provide.[37] This enchantment with chemicals is a poor substitute for stable trusting bonds.[38]

Trust-Wary Brains

I am still careful about whom I trust. People give off vibes and I can tell whether they are safe or not. If I see someone I don't think I can trust, I will use any excuse to stay away from that person. After being forced to talk about my problems, I have trouble relating to counselors and therapists. It seems like they are trying to act like my friend just so they can find out shit about me. I usually say, "Leave me the hell alone." Most just give up.[39] - Allan

While humans are naturally social, they also are vulnerable to being hurt or deceived. Thus, our social brains try to detect what the genuine intention of others might be. After about three years of age, children begin to develop the ability to imagine what is in the minds of others – this is called the theory of mind. With this mind-reading ability, they are able to navigate their social world.

Humans are both "one another's solace and one another's predators."[40] The brain decides in a blink who is friend or foe. From the first time humans meet, they make instantaneous judgments: good or bad, friendly or unfriendly, warm or cold. Our social brain determines when to trust and when to be wary. Deep brain programs trigger distrust of persons who do not seem genuine or those who try to become too friendly too fast. These protect us from those who might feign friendliness but wish us ill.[41]

Most lies are told with words but usually show in the eyes and face. Judges, mothers, detectives, and journalists are supposed to be able to sniff out lies. But experiments show even they cannot tell if children are lying.[42] It turns out that detecting deception is a right-brain specialty. The only natural lie detectors are stroke victims. People with aphasia – damage to the left sides of their brains – can spot lies solely through facial cues three quarters of the time. Folks with healthy brains are right only half the time.[43]

Children who have been rejected or traumatized become highly alert to cues of danger or rejection. They carry pain of the past in memory traces and are biased to expect hostility from others.[44] These trust-wary kids are in an approach-avoidance conflict; they desperately want to reach out for love, but they fear being hurt so back away.

Trust-wary youngsters adapt predictable coping strategies with adults in authority.[45] Some *fight* overtly by displaying defiance, opposition, antagonism, and rule-breaking behavior. Some use *flight* by becoming withdrawn, isolated, or lonely or by retreating into drug use or fantasy. Some use mechanisms to *fool* adults by masking their real feelings and manipulating, provoking, and outwitting adults. Predictably, since they are at odds with adults, these youth often gravitate to like-minded peers to find a substitute sense of safety or belonging. Often this peer group is composed of similar trust-wary youth which further insulates youth from adult influence.

Kids who distrust adults do not have some disorder but are using coping strategies to protect themselves against the *enemy*. Traditional reward punishment strategies have little leverage with such youth but only feed into past patterns of coercive adults fighting defiant youth.[46] Fortunately, there are specific methods which enable helpers to parry this resistance and form bonds of mutual respect.

The Ecology of Trust

Relationships in the child's ecology either provide support or produce strain. The most powerful approaches to prevention and intervention seek to mobilize the entire system of relationships to foster positive growth. Given the power of relationships, it is puzzling why these have not been the focal point for evaluating effective education and treatment. We believe it is essential to track these various types of relationships which can have a powerful impact on young people:[47]

1. *Positive relationships in the family, including not only parents but siblings and extended kin.* These are the most enduring sources of support as they transcend a lifetime.

2. *A positive relationship between the youth and other adult mentors in the school, church, or community.* This often can compensate for problems in family relationships.

3. *Positive peer relationships both in school and structured or non-structured group activities.* Communities are responsible for providing opportunities for positive peer influence.

4. *Effective teamwork relationships in schools and youth organizations.* This includes relationships among staff and with parents and family.

5. *Relationship between administrators and subordinates.* The type of leadership in any organization either fosters a sense of community or fuels continuing conflict.

6. *Relationships of youth to the broader community.* Young people need opportunities to participate in positive roles where they can make contributions to others.

A Chinese proverb suggests that wisdom lies in being as flexible as a willow on details but stalwart as a pine on principles. Our field has encountered a sometimes confusing array of methods, philosophies, and fads. It is important to keep our vision clearly set on the stalwart pines, those caring human relationships which provide the foundation for powerful change in the lives of children. In the words of Nicholas Hobbs:

> Trust between child and adult is essential, the foundation upon which all other principles rest, the glue that holds teaching and learning together, the beginning point for re-education.[48]

John: Daring to Trust

John Seita had been removed from his family at age eight and rejected all attempts of others to build relationships. By age twelve, he had sabotaged fifteen placements in foster homes or group settings. John was sent by the juvenile court to Starr Commonwealth in Michigan which might have been just another notch on his outwit-adults belt. Instead, he encountered a young youth worker who discovered how to build a trusting connection. Young John grew up to be Dr. John Seita, now a professor at Michigan State University and an author on resilience. John recalls an early encounter of daring to trust:

Mr. Lambert was a child care worker at Starr. I didn't know where he came from or really much about him except that he seemed sincere and reached out to me. It was his caring that set the stage for me to be where I am today. We met when I was thirteen. Starr had arranged for some of its residents to attend camp that summer at the University of Michigan Fresh Air Camp in Hell, Michigan. Hell is a small community in Michigan. Its curious name succinctly described my state of mind and spirit. I enjoyed the irony of it – spending time in Hell, that is. The real irony was that it wasn't *hell*. Meeting Mr. Lambert was a start of an intense and caring relationship. The timing of his reaching out to me was especially important since I had become increasingly lonely. I was still licking my emotional wounds from my numerous placements. I was wary, yet ready for someone or something better.

Our first meeting was near a lake at the camp. I had just given up trying to water ski and had belly flopped across Lake Hell after being scared to let go of the tow rope. Still stinging and aching all over, I plopped down on the sand. Mr. Lambert sat down beside me. He said something lighthearted about the less-than-successful water skiing adventure, being careful not to criticize my attempt at the sport. Then he said the magic word – baseball. "I don't know about you, John," he laughed, "but I think I prefer baseball to water skiing any day!" Just like that, Mr. Lambert had opened a chink in my armor. We started talking about baseball. Talking about baseball was my one means of reaching out to people. I would talk to almost anyone about baseball, no matter how angry I was.

Finally, I had lowered my personal line of defense and let an adult get close enough to care. Mr. Lambert shared many of the subtleties of life that one only learns at the elbow of a caring and experienced mentor. We fished at Starr's Montcalm Lake, played basketball, and he taught me about curiosity and critical thinking. In essence, this strong bond of connectedness formed the solid personal infrastructure for my life as a mature adult.[49]

[1] Glantz & Pearce, 1989, p. 205.

[2] Ratey, 2002, p. 302.

[3] Key, 1909.

[4] Baumeister & Leary, 1995.

[5] Lewis, Amini, & Lannon, 2001, p. 69.

[6] Brown, 1991.

[7] Taylor & Gonzaga, 2007.

[8] Johnston, 1999, p. 41.

[9] Lewis, Amini, & Lannon, 2000, p. 37.

[10] Way, 1993, p. 4.

[11] Erikson, 1977, p. 91.

[12] Konner, 2002.

[13] Erik Erikson, Abraham Maslow, John Bowlby, and Mary Ainsworth all put safety at the center of their theories.

[14] Carter, 2003; Taylor, 2002.

[15] Ratey, 2002.

[16] Nelson & Panksepp, 1998.

[17] Hofer, 1987; Wexler, 2006.

[18] Ratey, 2002.

[19] Konner, 2002.

[20] Carter, 2007.

[21] Cozolino, 2006, p. 322.

[22] Cozolino, 2006.

[23] Izard & Ackerman, 2000.

[24] Goleman, 2006.

[25] Mirror neurons were first discovered in research on monkeys by Italian scientists Rizzolatti and colleagues (1996). As monkeys picked up an object, the scientists performed brain scans. They observed that just before the motor area of the brain fired, a pre-motor region lit up, apparently sending the signal for action. But when the experimenter inadvertently picked up the object, the monkey's brain sent the same signal, mirroring the experimenter's behavior.

[26] Cozolino, 2006.

[27] Spindle cells are also called *von economo* neurons. They are most prominent in humans but some have been found in primates and whales.

[28] Cozolino, 2006.

[29] Bateson, Nettle, & Roberts, 2006.

[30] Carter, 1998.

[31] Cozolino, 2006.

[32] Provine, 2000.

[33] Bower, 2007.

[34] Genuine versus manipulated smiles are called Duchenne and non-Duchenne smiles respectively after the 19th century scientist [Guillaume Duchenne, 1806-1875] who discovered this distinction by placing pins in his face muscles and mapping their movements.

[35] Merker, 2007. This condition is called *hydranencephaly*.

[36] Foltz, 2008.

[37] Cozolino, 2006.

[38] Chambers, 2002.

[39] Brendtro & Shahbazian, 2003, p. 11.

[40] Taylor, 2002, p. 48.

[41] DeBecker, 1997.

[42] Ekman, 2001.

[43] Ecoff et al., 2000.

[44] Dodge & Somberg, 1987.

[45] Seita & Brendtro, 2005.

[46] Brendtro & Larson, 2006.

[47] Brendtro, 1985.

[48] Hobbs, 1982, p. 22.

[49] Seita, Mitchell, & Tobin, 1996, pp. 41-42.

CHAPTER FIVE

Challenge Maps

The motive for mastery lies at the heart of man's love for challenge.
But when the goal is attained, boredom – or even apathy –
replaces zeal and a new prize is sought.[1]

- Jerome Kagan -

IT WAS THE HARDEST THING SHE'D EVER BEEN ASKED TO DO. *How was she going to stand up in front of two hundred people and introduce the guest speaker? Ellen was chosen to speak because she had written the winning essay. But writing and speaking are two different things, she thinks. With sweaty palms and a dry mouth, Ellen hears her name called. As she rises, she sees her family seated in the audience. Her mother is smiling. I can do this, Ellen suddenly realizes. The young girl says a quick prayer, takes a sip of water and begins.*

Humans are problem solvers, but the human brain likes to create challenges as well. We only think when we are confronted with problems, said John Dewey. He noted that all problem solving begins with *felt difficulty*.[2] Today we would use the term stress. Humans function best when they are dealing with *just manageable difficulties*.[3] From early childhood, the brains of children seek a balance between security of the predictable and curiosity about the unknown.

Prepared for Mastery

Mastery is the drive to strengthen one's knowledge, skill, or talent.[4] The motivation to master challenges is universal across all human civilizations. Children everywhere watch elders and learn from them. In all cultures, persons use language and storytelling to describe past experiences. In their desire to make sense of their world, humans create theories to explain events and behavior and to understand the motivations of fellow beings.[5]

Children selectively imitate those to whom they are attached. For optimal development, they need to learn from models and mentors rather than rely on solo trial and error. The difference between the child's actual level of ability and the level he or she can achieve under the guidance of a mentor was called the *zone of proximal development* by Russian psychologist Vygotsky.[6] The most efficient learning comes from an interaction with a trusted person of greater ability. Mentors can be adults or more experienced peers.

In natural environments, children eagerly learn from elders and peers. Psychologists have long known that the desire to be competent is a preeminent human motivation.[7] In *task motivation*, the reward comes from improving one's performance. But, *egoistic motivation* involves comparing one's ability with others in the desire to be superior, as on an *ego trip*. This artificial system of motivation creates winners and losers without fostering an intrinsic love of learning. Egoistic motivation is the driving force in traditional schooling. The difference is very basic: Does one learn in order to beat others or to accomplish something?[8]

Intelligence is Resilience

Writing of learning and the brain, Robert Sylwester describes intelligence as "a person's ability to respond successfully to challenges and to learn from such experiences."[9] In other words, intelligence is resilience. As we master difficulties, we create new brain pathways, literally new intelligence. Brain imaging shows that persons who are considered expert in a certain area actually use less brain energy to solve problems than the novice. They are drawing on patterns etched in the deep brain. René Descartes put it this way: "Every problem that I solved became a rule which served afterwards to solve other problems."[10]

The brain is specifically designed to learn by coping with challenges. This process can be understood with the acronym CLEAR as shown in the

CLEAR Problem Solving

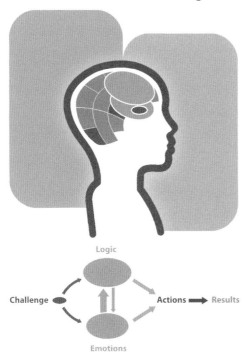

accompanying figure. Each problem-solving event begins with some **CHALLENGE** which triggers the amygdala. This information is then passed to brain centers for **LOGIC** as well as for **EMOTION**. The interplay of the higher and deeper brain systems leads to some **ACTION**. Coping behavior is designed to solve a problem or to manage emotions. This action achieves some **RESULT**, for better or worse.[11] As these patterns are repeated they form brain pathways for a particular style of coping with challenges.

By talking with youth about some challenging event, we can get a window into how they cope in either resilient or self-defeating ways. To understand behavior, it is helpful to know what stressful event triggered the sequence, what feelings and thoughts were activated, and what was the behavioral outcome. When youth have difficulty coping, it is often a case of distorted private logic which prevents the youth from making good decisions.

The greatest impediment to successful coping is not limited intelligence but a deep sense of inadequacy. Harvard educator Robert Brooks gives these examples of children who operate from the logic of helplessness and hopelessness:

> "I feel stupid. I feel I will never learn."
> "I can't think of anything I'm good at."
> "I was born with half a brain. Do you know how to fill in the other half?"[12]

Intelligence has many facets and we should assume that every young person has a hidden kernel of genius. Brooks challenges us to locate these strengths even in struggling students who seem to be drowning in failure. "If there are oceans of inadequacy, there must be islands of competence – areas that have been or have potential to be sources of pride and accomplishment."[13]

Successful life adjustment requires a unique kind of competence separate from school smarts. Robert Sternberg[14] identifies three types of intelligence: 1) *creative intelligence* involves new ways of doing things; 2) *analytic intelligence* is used to solve problems and to make judgments; and 3) *practical intelligence* is an intuitive ability to confront and solve problems in our everyday life and relationships. The term *street smart* comes to mind. This practical intelligence is often overlooked in schools where success is limited to narrow academics.

Most of the world's cultures have broader definitions of intelligence than the test-driven trivial pursuit of current Western society. Researchers who ask people to define intelligence in their own words discover three strong themes: the ability to communicate, the ability to solve practical problems, and the ability to get along with other people. The emphasis on social aspects of intelligence is much more common in Asian and African traditions than in Western culture.

An individualistic approach to learning fails to tap into the power of the social brain. Cooperative learning optimizes achievement, and groups perform better than individuals on a wide range of tasks.[15] Small groups come up with better solutions to problems than even bright individuals working alone. Three persons working together is usually enough to activate this superior group problem-solving ability.

A century ago, Jane Addams called for schools and youth programs which would capture the adventuresome spirit of youth.[16] This turns out to be brain-friendly learning since novelty is the brain's cue that some stimulus deserves our interest. Novelty is rewarding as long as it is not too strange, at which point it becomes threat. When short of novelty, the brain seeks out excitement or turns inward to fantasy. Adolescents seek new experiences and risk as a way of developing and defining themselves. Schools that capture this adventurous spirit create powerful learning.[17]

Play constructs new neural pathways, so brains actually grow during recess![18] Humans play more extensively and in more complex ways than all other species. Children play profusely and this activity enhances growth of nerve cells. Play also may foster the development of the frontal lobe, which involves planning and inhibiting action. This area is less well developed in kids with ADHD. Their immature brains may need more rough and tumble play to develop brain control systems. Ironically, drugs that reduce motor activity may produce short-term calming while inhibiting the very brain structures necessary for self-control. Throughout the lifespan, play activity enables the brain to continue developing new networks.

Deep Conversations

Children need adults in order to make meaning out of the challenges of their lives. Certainly most adults want to instill positive values in young persons. Yet it is remarkable that our hectic modern lifestyle has so few opportunities for these deep conversations. In contrast, children in tribal cultures have ongoing thoughtful exchanges with elders, both when things are going well and in times of difficulty. In traditional indigenous cultures, many different elders share the responsibility of engaging children who present behavioral problems in thoughtful conversations. As with any learning, practice is essential.

> Only reflective thinking can develop reflective thinking. The only way we can learn to walk is to practice walking, and the only way to mature our frontal lobes is to practice reflective problem-solving and advanced social skills that our frontal lobes regulate – even though young people are not very successful with it initially.[19]

Our goal is to connect youth to deep values rather than memorize rules. Teens crave excitement and thrills and, in the company of their peers, often make risky decisions.[20] Traditional prevention programs focus on *education* to give youth the necessary facts to make good decisions. As it turns out, this may be a weak strategy. Most adolescents already have well-developed logical brains – try winning an argument with a teen. They also intellectually understand the risk of certain behavior, such as reckless driving, drugs, and unsafe sex. But the payoff of peer approval and the absence of a long-term view make them vulnerable to risky behavior.[21]

While adolescents are *smart*, their brains are not yet *wise*. Research by Reyna and Farley[22] shows that at adolescence, the reasoning brain races past other brain systems. Teens have newfound logical abilities to debate what they should believe and do. They abandon child-like obedience before their teen brains are equipped to make wise decisions.

When these researchers asked such questions as "Is it a good idea to set your hair on fire?" or "Is it a good idea to drink a bottle of Drano?" teens take twice as long as adults to come up with the answer! They get sidetracked playing around with their newly minted logical brain and completely lose the big picture.

Contrary to common opinion, teens do not believe that they are invulnerable. In fact, they are likely to over-estimate the odds of bad outcomes, such as contracting venereal disease or dying in an accident. But reasoning is an inadequate basis for preventing risk-taking behavior. Only deeply internalized values will give these young people a moral compass.

Until youth are mature, adults are responsible for removing risks they cannot yet handle. Kids lacking impulse control need more guidance and mentoring to reduce risks. It is not sufficient to encourage sound thinking and problem solving; the environments in which adolescents develop must also be modified to remove opportunities for unhealthy risk taking when adolescents are not ready to handle them.[23]

Problems as Opportunity

Crisis events can provide powerful learning because the brain is primed to record these experiences. These pivotal teaching moments can build social and emotional competency. Neuroscientist Sue Taylor explains:

> Although most children are taught to be nice to people, what they are taught to do when their emotions are at fever pitch and their stress systems are throbbing matters a good deal more to their developing social skills and future behavior.[24]

Moral development researcher Martin Hoffman proposed that problems be handled as learning opportunities through *inductive discipline*. This is an alternative to discipline using *power assertion* or *love withdrawal*. As young people form inductions about how their behavior affects others, they gain empathy and pro-social values.[25]

Hoffman believes that a limitation of many attempts at training character was the narrow focus on one dimension – only behavior or thinking or emotion. Natural emotionally-charged life experiences can tap into all these learning processes.

Hoffman's research suggests that the most effective discipline methods involve *scripts* to help children organize experience and guide future actions. These messages are of a level of complexity matched to the child's maturity. With recurring problems, we have fresh opportunities to replay scripts and reinforce deep brain values.

While scripts need not be preaching, youth must recognize if they have hurt another person and feel appropriate guilt for their actions. For example in peer helping groups, the message *everyone helps, nobody hurts* is invoked repeatedly in various iterations until it becomes internalized.

Hoffman cautions that verbal interventions are only effective in the context of a supportive relationship. Further, since extreme distress interferes with reasoning, this requires calming emotions so verbal communication will be effective. Certainly, adults may at times need to use some power

Response Ability Pathways

CONNECT
*with persons
in need*

CLARIFY
*challenges
and problems*

RESTORE
*harmony and
respect*

From Brendtro & du Toit, 2005.

assertion to get an individual to stop, pay attention, and communicate about this problem.

The concept of using problems as teachable moments is the foundation of three life space intervention models: Response Ability Pathways [RAP], Life Space Crisis Intervention [LSCI], and Positive Peer Culture [PPC].[26] RAP is a universal training built on resilience and neuroscience principles. This approach prepares mentors to help youth cope in responsible ways with the normal challenges they encounter. Everyday events become the grist for building resilience. RAP is a three-stage problem-solving process as summarized in the accompanying figure. This involves *Connecting* for support, *Clarifying* challenges, and *Restoring* balance by meeting the Circle of Courage needs for Belonging, Mastery, Independence, and Generosity.

Life Space Crisis Intervention

Life Space Crisis Intervention provides advanced therapeutic strategies to use problems as opportunities for growth and healing.[27] LSCI adds a diagnostic process to identify six patterns of self-defeating behavior as listed on the following page.[28] An adult and youth examine the time line of some crisis event or conflict cycle. This provides information on the young person's characteristic style of thinking, feeling, and behaving. LSCI is a therapy model that can be incorporated with RAP or other individual or peer group approaches.

1. Imported problems: *This intervention is for youngsters who carry in problems from home or street and displace their distress on others. The goal is to manage problems and gain positive support.* **Developing self-control and support fosters mastery and belonging.**

2. Errors in perception: *These problems arise from distortions in thinking or perception that lead to maladaptive behavior. The goal is to help a youth think clearly and understand reality.* **Developing clear thinking fosters mastery and responsibility.**

3. Delinquent pride: *This involves students who are purposely aggressive and exploit others but do not feel appropriate guilt for their behavior. The goal is to help a youth feel empathy and concern for others.* **Developing empathy fosters generosity.**

4. Impulsivity and guilt: *This involves youth who feel guilty about impulsive acts but lack confidence or self-worth. The goal is to strengthen inner controls on behavior.* **Developing self-control fosters independence.**

5. Limited social skills: *This involves youth who have appropriate motivation but lack the tools for success. The goal is to teach specific skills that enhance the youth's coping ability.* **Developing social skills can help the youth meet belonging, mastery, and other needs.**

6. Vulnerability to peer influence: *This involves youth who let peers manipulate them into destructive behaviors. The goal is to manage self without being a pawn of peers.* **Developing inner control fosters independence.**

Peer Problem Solving

I think it helps the most just to talk to people your own age that are going through the same stuff and you can connect with them.[31] - Jerry

     Positive Peer Culture or PPC uses peer helping to guide youth towards responsible behavior. To facilitate this process, students meet regularly in formal peer helping groups with an adult facilitator called the *group leader* or *coach*.

They are enlisted in caring for others rather than just being passive recipients of care. Members learn to provide one another helpful feedback and support.

PPC groups often use a problem-solving list to define and highlight behavior that hurts self or others. Problems are presented in light of the positive strengths needed to resolve them as shown in the accompanying list. Helping skills learned in group sessions are applied to the natural everyday life of youth. Service projects extend helping beyond the peer group to the broader community.

Unlike group models that unleash peer confrontation, PPC focuses on building trust among youth and with staff. A cohesive group is formed to spark natural empathy and helping behavior. These groups are effective both with buoyant and resilient youth but also those who are beset and troubled. In a safe, supportive group, even vulnerable youth like those with diagnoses of Asperger's syndrome, depression, and trauma can get help. Staff trained in RAP, LSCI, or other therapy models can augment group effectiveness.

Turning Problems into Strengths

Problems	Strengths
Low self image	Confident
Inconsiderate of others	Respect others
Inconsiderate of self	Respect self
Authority problem	Cooperative
Misleads others	Positive leadership
Easily misled	Self determination
Aggravate others	Social competence
Easily angered	Emotional control
Stealing	Trustworthy
Alcohol or drug abuse	Clear headed
Lying	Honest
Fronting	Genuine

John Gibbs and colleagues have expanded PPC to EQUIP youth as more effective peer helpers.[32] Parallel with peer helping groups, youth receive formal training in cognitive moral development, managing emotions, and social skills. This attention to the triad of thinking, emotions, and behavior draws on a strong research base and contributes to the model's consilience.

thinking hazards

BAMMS
Thinking Errors

Blaming
*Others always start
fights with me.
I'm worthless and don't
deserve to live.*

Assuming the worst
*You can't trust anyone.
They lie to you.
No matter how hard I try,
I always fail.*

Minimizing &
Mislabeling
*Everyone does it,
what's the big deal?
So I slapped her around.
She's such a slut.*

Self-centered
*If I see something I like,
then it's mine.
Why do I care?
I look out for number one.*

From Gibbs, Potter & Goldstein
EQUIP Model

Exploring thinking distortions is now standard practice in PPC programs. Youth not only identify problem behavior but identify the *thinking errors* that spark and maintain problems. Left unchallenged, distorted private logic can block empathy and justify hurting behavior. Most youth know the difference between good and bad but need to strengthen deep brain programs that motivate pro-social behavior.[33] Targeting distorted thinking helps youth explore how their thinking and behavior impacts self and others.

Youth are taught to spot these errors called BAMMS, an acronym for five most common distortions. As shown here, thinking hazards include blaming others, assuming the worst, minimizing, mislabeling, and self-centered thinking. The last is the foundation of all thinking errors. As youth are challenged to show care and concern for others, helping overrides hurting.

Adventure Learning

Instead of fighting the natural motivation of youth for risk and adventure, this spirit can be tapped and channeled. Such programs are highly intense and usually last a few weeks rather than the longer placements typical of residential treatment. Students in the Montcalm Adventure Challenge Program at Starr Commonwealth go through this process of growth and change:

Getting a Fresh Start. As youth enter the program, they leave behind the familiar and confront the challenges of coping with a new environment.

They learn the basic skills to live simply in nature among a close community of peers and staff. Students begin to clear their minds of previous distractions and patterns of thinking and behavior. As youth build trust with their group, they share their personal life story. They have an opportunity to send an impact letter to their family which will be followed by counseling sessions. With the support of staff, peers, and their family, youth reflect on their problems and goals and begin to develop an individual growth plan.

Exploring New Possibilities. Youth develop growing competence to cope effectively within the primitive natural world and in their network of interpersonal relationships. They acquire new skills in coping with social, academic, and physical challenge. They strengthen innate abilities for communication, cooperation, and problem-solving. Now more aware of the emotions of self and others, they become effective helpers of peers, demonstrating empathy and genuine concern.

Transformational Change. During the final stage, young people demonstrate growing responsibility and begin to make true value changes. As they reach beyond themselves to help create and inspire change in others, they have opportunity to continue developing and internalizing their own personal growth skills. They develop a plan with specific goals for their future life pathways.

Positive Psychology

The dawn of the 21st century resurrected the earlier spirit of optimism of youth work pioneers. The American Psychological Association formally shifted its focus beyond deficits toward character strengths and virtues.[34] There was now a research base for the strength-based movement, namely resilience science. But this approach is also an issue of personal values. Those who fail to see strengths and potentials in troubled youth will always believe coercion is essential and empowerment is naïve.

The strength-based philosophy holds that all persons have natural abilities to cope with challenges, although these might be masked by self-defeating behaviors. The goal is to find and develop latent potentials. Successful coping allows young people to take pathways to positive youth development. Surmounting challenges builds strengths. Resilience research and neuroscience show that young people can overcome trauma and mistreatment and become stronger in the process.

Resilience is not in short supply but is part of the human DNA. We build the strengths of resilience by opportunities for Belonging, Mastery, Independence, and Generosity.[35] These four strengths broadly correspond to the structure of character strengths identified in research on positive psychology by Chris Peterson of the University of Michigan.[36]

The most extensive studies of resilience were conducted in Hawaii by Emmy Werner and Ruth Smith.[37] They tracked children at risk across three decades of life. Most had many problems during childhood and into young adulthood. But, by their thirties, a majority were able to cope effectively, regardless of risk factors or earlier problems. When followed up after maturity, a significant number of participants refused to accept a modest twenty dollar stipend; they were appreciative for just having been included in this study.

The number of caring adults outside the family was a major predictor for success in high risk youngsters. During adolescence, a caring teacher or other mentor helped these youth succeed against the odds. School success was also a powerful buffer against adversity. And many developed a sense of spiritual purpose by contributing to their family and community. The researchers concluded:

> Most of all, self-esteem and self-efficacy were promoted through supportive relationships. The youngsters in our study had at least one person in their lives who accepted them unconditionally, regardless of temperamental idiosyncrasies, physical attractiveness, or intelligence.[38]

Decades of research show that school performance strongly impacts the course of young lives. Even if other areas of life are disrupted, positive experiences in school have their own transformational effect. On the other hand, school failure itself is a significant contributor to poor life adjustment and to delinquent behavior.[39] No other role in our society is as fraught with potential failure as student-hood. School failure or rejection by peers and teachers derogates self-worth; delinquent behavior, particularly disruption at school, is a defense against this failure.

Martin Gold has researched extensively effective alternative schools. While they differ widely, two attributes are essential. First, students are not permitted to fail. Second, staff members provide a great deal of warm personal support. Gold found that effective alternative schools were able to flexibly adapt curriculum and discipline procedures to meet the needs of students at risk. Such flexibility is less common in regular schools where rules and consequences may be doled out with unbending consistency. Some principals even believe it is their job to purge or push out troublemakers.[40]

Herman McCall followed students from Starr Commonwealth's alternative schools into regular education in the community.[41] His research focused on students who succeeded in alternative schools but later dropped out of regular schools. It became clear that those who disengaged lacked positive, supportive relationships with most regular school personnel. The prevailing practice of trying to return all alternative students to regular settings needs to be questioned if the regular school is unable to provide the academic and interpersonal support needed for success.

When these students failed, there were discrepant theories of blame. School officials typically attributed the cause to *poor parenting*. The main reason given by students themselves was *poor treatment*. There is some indication that students who fail are more likely to be of the *beset* type who anticipate and sometimes contribute to their own rejection.

McCall concluded that school personnel will need positive training experiences if they are to be equipped to meet the needs of troubled students. Such training would address key components such as these:

Turning problems into opportunities. Staff need specific skills to disengage from conflict and connect with reluctant students. Training in recognizing conflict cycles is central to building safe and reclaiming schools. Research shows that 90 per cent of teachers do not feel competent to handle crisis or talk with children in times of conflict.[42] Such training is now available and should be part of the competency of school personnel.[43]

Creating cultural safety. The fact that minority youth are over-represented in school discipline and disengagement provides a clue to action, although it has been fashionable to sweep this unpleasant reality under the carpet. James Kauffman suggests that we will need more than understanding diversity to discover what binds us together. He proposes the Circle of Courage model for organizing schools around super-ordinate goals of Belonging, Mastery, Independence, and Generosity.[44] The Institutes for Healing Racism provide another promising avenue for discovering the oneness of humankind.[45] Unless children from diverse backgrounds experience what Maori educators call "cultural safety," they will continue departing in droves.

Creating respectful school climates. Marginalized students are drawn to other peers who also feel like outcasts. School climate research shows that when students at risk encounter hostile peer and staff cultures, problems are exacerbated. Depressed kids become more desperate; oppositional kids become more defiant; and conduct problem kids engage in more antisocial behavior.[46] There are large numbers of alienated students in our schools, and educators alone cannot be expected to solve all of their problems. We need more than some add-on program to *mediate conflict* or *bully-proof* schools. The solution is to create climates of belonging in our schools. In these settings, all students and staff join together in the pursuit of mastery.

Adie: School as Anchor

Adie was homeless and deeply lonely, but her alternative school provided stability and trusting bonds.

As hard as living on the streets was for me, it was easier than being at home and putting up with the abuse. At least I had control over what was happening to me most of the time. I felt my parents got rid of me because

I was not good enough. My friends pushed me away because I was not good enough. I was not good enough for anybody out there.

You develop such a low self-esteem being pushed away from your own family. It's a rejection thing. You are going through all of this hardship and your family should comfort you, but they don't. When you are at home and you've got parents, you've got support and attention and everything you need. I had no stability, no love, no affection, and I had no one to talk to. I had no one.

If you can't trust and rely on your own parents, well, who can you turn to? Your whole view of the world is shattered. Even to this day, I am learning to trust people.

School gave me a sense of stability. I felt like I was normal going to school every day when I could. Having people there who I know and someone I trusted. It made me feel better about myself. Even though I don't have anyone when I am on my own, I could go the next day if I needed to talk to someone. That's what I actually lived for, to go to school.[47]

[1] Condensed from Kagan, 1971, p. 54.

[2] Dewey, 1910.

[3] Hobbs, 2007.

[4] Kagan, 1971.

[5] Brown, 1991.

[6] Lev Vygotsky [1896-1934], cited in VanderVen, 2003.

[7] White, 1959.

[8] Nicholls, 1990.

[9] Sylwester, 2005, p. 87.

[10] Descartes, 1637.

[11] While cognitive psychologists often emphasize how logic controls emotion and behavior, it appears that even our deliberate decisions are prefabricated in the deep brain seconds before we consciously act on them (Gazzaniga, 2008).

[12] Brooks, 2007, p. 11.

[13] Brooks, 2007, p. 11.

[14] Sternberg, 1996.

[15] Laughlin et al., 2006.

[16] Addams, 1909.

[17] Strother, 2007.

[18] Bergen, 2006.

[19] Sylwester, 2005, p. 78.

[20] Reyna & Farley, 2006.

[21] Gardner & Steinberg, 2005.

[22] Reyna & Farley, 2006.

[23] Reyna & Farley, 2006, p. 18.

[24] Taylor, 2002, p. 69.

[25] Hoffman, 2002.

[26] Regular features on these methods are carried in the quarterly journal *Reclaiming Children and Youth*. See www.reclaiming.com.

[27] Brendtro & Long, 2005.

[28] Long, Wood, & Fecser, 2001.

[29] Brendtro, du Toit, Bath, & Van Bockern, 2007.

[30] Koehler, 2007.

[31] Woodland Hills Students, 1993, p. 7.

[32] Gibbs, Potter, & Goldstein, 1995; Gibbs, Potter, DiBiase, & Devlin, in press.

[33] Blair, Mitchell, & Blair, 2005; Newman, 1998.

[34] Seligman & Czikszentmihalyi, 2000; Peterson & Seligman, 2004.

[35] Brendtro & Larson, 2006.

[36] Peterson, 2008.

[37] Werner & Smith, 1992.

[38] Werner & Smith, 1992, p. 205.

[39] Gold, 1995.

[40] Fine, 1991.

[41] McCall, 2003.

[42] Dawson, 2003.

[43] Long, Wood, & Fecser, 2001; Brendtro, Ness, & Mitchell, 2005.

[44] Kauffman, 2000.

[45] Newkirk & Rutstein, 2000.

[46] Hyman & Snook, 1999.

[47] Excerpted from Glasson-Walls, 2004.

CHAPTER SIX

Power Maps

You may encounter many defeats, but you must not be defeated.[1]

- Maya Angelou -

EVER SINCE THEY WERE KIDS, SCOTT HAS BEEN THE LEADER AND TED, THE SIDEKICK. *Ted admires his friend's confidence and courage and is proud to be known as Scott's best friend. But now, in middle school, things are changing. Scott isn't content playing kickball and riding bikes anymore. At their neighborhood convenience store, Scott elbows Ted to show him a pack of gum he's pocketed. You get something, too, whispers Scott. Ted is conflicted. Should he follow his friend or make his own decisions?*

In every culture, people value being able to control their own lives and influence others.[2] All major theories of personality attest to the importance of autonomy, which is defined as the natural need to exert personal power and resist unwanted influence or coercion.[3] Autonomy is seen in diverse forms including the desire for freedom, responsibility, and independence, and the resistance to external control. Autonomy is balanced by the need to belong to a group and our tendency to follow strong or admired leaders. When this motive towards power is not properly socialized, the result is the unbridled aggression or a sense of helplessness.

Developing Autonomy

From earliest childhood, children exert their fledgling power. Play itself is an act of autonomy. Rough and tumble mock-fighting is universal in young mammals. It is seldom violent as the young are just practicing their newly minted power.[4]

Martin Brokenleg has described how traditional Native American cultures encourage even very young children to make decisions, solve problems, and show personal responsibility – all the while keeping them interdependent with the community.[5] To interfere with a child's will is seen as disrespect unless behavior is harmful to self or others, in which case, elders teach proper responses. A similar approach is practiced by the Aka of Central Africa:

> Training for autonomy begins in infancy…Only if an infant begins to crawl into a fire or hits another child do parents or others interfere with the infant's activity… By three or four years of age, children can cook themselves a meal on the fire and by ten years of age, Aka children know enough subsistent skills to live in the forest alone if need be.[6]

Western philosophies of education and child rearing grew from a millennium of experience in autocratic cultures. The assumption was that children mainly learned through external application of rewards and punishments. But research shows that these obedience training models impede the development of self responsibility. Imposed goals, high-stakes evaluation, sanctions, and surveillance all undermine intrinsic motivation.[7] These of course are strategies used to pressure and control people. Certainly, external controls may be necessary until children develop controls from within. However, whether in school or the workplace, coercive strategies stifle enthusiasm and motivation.

The quest for autonomy surges with the onset of adolescence. Children of every age show a robust desire to be their own person, to do their own thing. However, this basic need intensifies in adolescence, which by its very nature is a prep course for independence. The Search Institute found that autonomy as measured by items like "I make my own decisions" increases more than any other value in early adolescence. Another goal that gains prominence during this period is "to do something important with my life." Humans want to make a difference in the world.[8]

One of the most novel ways to study youth in their natural environment is the Experience Sampling Method (ESM).[9] Teens are hired to carry pagers throughout their waking hours. At random times, they are paged and complete questionnaires on precisely what they were doing, thinking, and feeling.

For most, their greatest time is when they are with peers, following their own interests without adult control. When paged in school, most students are trying to concentrate, but this is related to getting grades but not to any intrinsic interest in learning. Even studies of talented students show this pattern since most schools do not build internal motivation.[10] Because of test requirements, teachers try to cover as much ground as possible rather than engage students as autonomous learners.

Power in the Brain

Humans have an inbuilt motivation to exert power and, at the most personal level, power equals autonomy. Every person desires to be in control of him- or herself. But humans are also social animals so whenever they come together, they need some mechanism to distribute personal power.

The lower brain offers a quick and simple answer – dominate or submit. Whenever animals encounter a stressful social situation, primitive power programs kick in. The amygdala instantly reads nonverbal cues to determine whether dominance or submission is the best option.[11] As they mature, children use social emotions that provide more information about their status in the group, such as pride, contempt, shame, and humiliation.[12]

Nonverbal signs of dominance and submission are related to the fight-flight response.[13] Dominance is expressed through displays to make one loom larger and more intimidating. Puff up, chest out, swagger, scowl, and growl. Such power displays are associated with higher levels of testosterone, which is related to dominance, social status, and aggression. Even in the absence of threat displays, our brains are designed to take note of size and strength. Children *look up to* adults and are inclined to defer to their power. Tall persons are historically overrepresented among political leaders. Since the elderly no longer project physical power but are essential to survival of culture, our brains may even defer to silver hair as a sign of strength.

Nonverbal signs of submission are tied to brain cues that indicate one's social status. In the primitive program of the amygdala, big is interpreted as dangerous and small is safe. Thus, submission is tied to acting small and unthreatening, sometimes feigning friendliness.[14] Avert eyes, look meek and vulnerable, shrink in size – such behaviors signal that one acknowledges, complies with, or surrenders to the power of another. The message is clear: I will not be a threat to your power. In these contests for status, dominance and victory raise the level of testosterone. The loser in this power struggle has lower levels of testosterone, biological priming for a role of submission.[15]

While submission and dominance programs are normal and essential for social harmony, they can create intense personal pain and social conflict when they go awry. Two extremes are the powerlessness of learned helplessness and the displaced power of learned defiance.

Learned Helplessness

When children have no opportunity to exercise personal power, the temporary *state* of submission can turn into a pervasive *trait*. Such children experience deep feelings of inferiority and inadequacy. They have little confidence that they can improve their lives or impact the world. This mindset of powerlessness has been called learned helplessness.[16] Such persons have been trained to falsely believe that they have no power to control their environment. For example, they might resign themselves to accept abuse rather than take action to change their life circumstances.

Helplessness is often associated with pessimistic thinking and depression. Children's private logic about the world is more powerful than reality. It is how one interprets events rather than reality itself that best predicts one's self-concept, goals, academic performance, and mental health.[17] In fact, holding somewhat inflated notions of one's abilities seems to contribute to healthy development and adjustment.[18] Thus, an antidote to learned helplessness is learned optimism which is a characteristic of resilience.

The core problem underlying learned helplessness is a lack of self-efficacy as extensively researched by Albert Bandura.[19] Self-efficacy is a person's sense of one's own capabilities, strength, or power to achieve desired goals. Again, it is not just our real ability, but our beliefs about our ability that count. "With the same set of skills, people may perform poorly, adequately, or extraordinarily depending upon their self beliefs of efficacy."[20]

No area of the brain is uniquely involved in self-efficacy. Rather, deeply embedded memories of success or failure prepare us to attack and solve problems or to retreat in learned helplessness. "Those who believe they cannot manage potential threats experience high levels of stress. They judge themselves as highly vulnerable and view many aspects of their environment as fraught with danger."[21] This conditioned fear of failure overwhelms the ability to cope. In its most extreme form, helplessness in the face of some terrifying life event is the foundation of trauma.[22]

Self-efficacy is courage in encountering challenge. It may be even more crucial than a positive self-image. While self-worth is based on how we feel about ourselves, self-efficacy is the confidence we have in our abilities. The primary way of building self-efficacy is a history of success which breeds success. Studies show that when teachers strengthen self-efficacy, students make gains equivalent of moving from the fiftieth to the seventieth percentile.[23]

Bandura describes various ways to build self-efficacy.[24] Children need mastery experiences. This does not mean quick success but the courage to fail and rebound from setbacks. They need models for resilience. Seeing persons similar to oneself succeed through effort raises beliefs about one's own efficacy. Of course, seeing others like oneself fail can stir self doubt. Young people also need encouragement and positive expectations that call forth their potentials for self-responsibility. Finally, they need opportunities likely to bring success, and protection from experiences likely to lead to repeated failures.

Self-efficacy is a linchpin to self-responsibility. With social support and brain maturation, most youth display considerable responsibility by about seventeen years of age.[25] Responsible youth believe that they can depend on themselves, assert themselves, and resist negative influence. They have perspective about the long-term effects of their actions on themselves and on others. Responsible youth gain self-control as they manage impulsivity and regulate their emotions. These young people are confident in their ability to make responsible decisions to achieve important life goals.

Learned Defiance

Fritz Redl chronicled various causes of defiance to show that catch-all terms like *aggression* or *violence* lack precision.[26] Such descriptors lump together a wide variety of *fight* behaviors that have little in common except that someone devalues these expressions of power. Acts of aggression can range from self defense to predatory behavior, from hate-filled revenge to impulsive rage, from protecting my homeland to invading yours.

All humans by nature are self protective and capable of both fight and flight. But we are not by nature aggressive unless provoked or backed in a corner – or unless something in our developmental experience or brain controls has gone awry. For whatever reason, males who are threatened are more likely to react with fight reactions while women are inclined to seek safety in attachments.[27]

At the most basic level, researchers distinguish between reactive and proactive aggression. The first is an emotionally charged defense against perceived threat. The second includes unprovoked, pre-meditated aggression to achieve personal gain.[28] Reactive aggression probably results from amygdala alarm triggering the defensive right brain, while proactive aggression entails calculated actions using the logic and approach circuits of the left brain.

Reactive aggression in children was attributed by Richard Jenkins to early rejection.[29] These emotionally damaged youth were called *beset* by Martin Gold to differentiate them from more resilient and *buoyant* youth.[30]

Beset children grow up in emotionally hazardous relationships and environments that lay down brain pathways making knee-jerk aggression the standard survival style.

A less recognized strain of reactive aggression is fueled by cultures or communities where a real or imagined sense of danger is met with a "don't tread on me" mentality. Deep values that restrain or fuel aggression can be transmitted across generations. The forgiveness shown by Amish when an outsider massacred their children shows the ability of moral values to reign in violence. In contrast, fighting at any sign of disrespect is a norm in some subcultures. Many of our students from the streets of Detroit have hair-trigger reactions to being dissed.

Researchers argue whether social bonding or self control is the primary prevention against delinquency and violence. In fact, social bonding is the only way the brain is able to build self-control. Restorative interventions provide a direct means of rebuilding social bonds and thus strengthening self control. However, many *get tough* practices in schools and the justice system further disrupt social bonds which render these as weak interventions.[31]

Redl describes the key reasons youth learn to show defiance. All are related to the failure to meet the most basic developmental needs. 1) The child who has been hurt or violated fights adults and has no reason to identify with authority or their values. 2) The child who has not developed ego skills cannot cope with challenges but gets stuck in conflict cycles and self-defeating behavior. 3) The youth who lacks opportunity to express growing needs for independence shows an *intelligent rebellion* and fights external controls. 4) A final type of youth has built his or her identity around an impulsive and self-centered life style. The youngster shows little empathy or silences the small voice of conscience with distortions in thinking. Redl saw this last type of youth as presenting the most serious problems because they evoke hostility rather than support from adults who deal with them.

Both learned helplessness and learned defiance represent a *dance of disturbance* between young people and others in their immediate world.

Bioecological science shows that the most direct way to change children's lives is to change the nature of relationships with significant adults and peers. As Andrew Ross explains, schools and youth organizations need to transform their cultures to be compatible with how the child's brain works.[32] These powerful environments operate in moment by moment experiences to build deeply embedded pathways for pro-social thinking and behavior. In the remainder of this chapter we highlight some of the specifics of creating powerful cultures for learning.

Beyond Rankism

Our primitive survival brain determines rank through the rules of raw power, dominate or submit. But the higher social brain of humans has a better alternative. This recognizes that all persons are endowed with a desire for self-determination. Thus power must be reigned in by brain programs for mutual empathy and respect.

In social groups, some leaders gain the respect of others because they are admired for positive traits such as competence, compassion, and the ability to inspire cooperation. Others grab power through intimidation or aggression. Democratic cultures monitor the process by which people rise to the top and put limits on the power of those who gain such rank.[33]

In his book *Somebodies and Nobodies*, former college president Robert Fuller described his experience tutoring school dropouts in math. These students believed they were nobodies in schools that devalued their importance. He found he could teach them math only when he treated them as somebodies. All of us have had experiences of being treated as nobodies and we resent it. Fuller coined a new term to describe this generic misuse of power: rankism.[34]

Treating others as nobodies is rankism. Rankism is the demeaning behavior of any individual in a position of power. Rankism occurs when persons in power *pull rank* and use their position to bully or exclude others. Rankism has been called the mother of all isms. Racism, sexism, ageism, and all such pseudo superiority mindsets are rankism. Whenever we treat another as less than our social equal, we show rankism.

There is nothing wrong with high rank based on merit. We want our doctors and teachers, sports teams and orchestras to have persons with high talent. The problem is when anyone uses power to hurt rather than to help and serve.

Patterns of rankism are vestiges of pre-democratic Western culture. They are perpetuated in coercive practices of behavior management in family, school, or community. While this is not a book on discipline, all effective programs for youth must break free of these entrenched but failed assumptions. We illustrate this with examples from recent research on coercive discipline.

The Language of Disrespect

Respect and disrespect are built in thousands of daily micro-communications of respect or indignity. Ramon Lewis of Melbourne, Australia, has studied thousands of students in secondary schools worldwide.[35] He found that sarcasm and group humiliation were common with stressed-out teachers who lacked positive discipline strategies. However, when teachers used such methods, students actually behaved in less responsible ways. While students widely ridicule one another, they place much higher expectations on adults in this regard than they would on peers. Thus it is very easy for persons in authority to slip into rather mild humor or sarcasm that is deeply humiliating to children – specifically because of the rank held by the teacher.

Irwin Hyman, who headed the School Psychology Division of the American Psychological Association, has documented how experiences in schools can create enduring trauma in many students. Through an instrument called the My Worst School Experience Scale, he found that sixty per cent of the most traumatic events reported by students were related to peer ridicule and mistreatment. But he was astounded to find that forty per cent of these destructive encounters were with school staff. For example, a student reported:

One day in Spanish class, I told the teacher I was lost and didn't know what was going on; in reply he said, "There is a place for people like you to go and it's called the 'lost and found.'" The whole class laughed but to me it wasn't funny and I was embarrassed.[36]

Sarcasm is a thinly veiled hostility, a form of passive aggressive rankism.[37] It has the same intent as more direct verbal insults, namely, to demean the self-worth of the targeted individual. The old sticks and stones metaphor has been buried by brain science. In fact, words are the most powerful weapons to create deep shame, perhaps the most powerful of negative emotions.

Our brains are highly attuned to social rejection and are equipped with a sarcasm detector.[38] This is how it works. For example, a teacher says to a distracted student, "Glad to see you are working so diligently." To spot the real meaning of this remark, the frontal brain cross checks the "compliment" decoded by the left brain with the sarcastic tone and presumed intent of the speaker. Sarcasm treads a fine line between harsh humor and cutting contempt. It allows the attacker to hide behind polite words while throwing emotional daggers. Groups also use sarcasm to demean outsiders and to put down authority figures.[39]

These small attacks are called micro-insults. The insulter may not even be conscious of the message being delivered. Micro-insults were first described in research on racism but these indignities permeate all types of rankism.[40] For example, direct name calling was common in old-fashioned racism and is prevalent in school bullying. Attacks may be public or behind the back of the person. Other micro-insults demean a person's heritage or identity. Comments disparaging *today's teens* fill the public discourse. Political rhetoric such as attacking *illegal* immigrants or berating affirmative action convey a profound message to those in the target group that they are unwanted and lack ability. Referring to one's family as dysfunctional or criticizing the *crazy* interests of teens only builds gulfs between groups of people. Non-verbal micro-insults such as rolling eyes, turning away, and shunning closeness erode self-worth. Some may feel that these examples are no big deal and kids need to just buck up and take it. However, microassaults are a big deal because these fuel anger and ruin relationships.

Rethinking Discipline

Punishment is vastly overrated as a behavioral intervention with troubled youth. It fails to build values in delinquent youth and it reactivates rejection in youngsters with a history of maltreatment. But it is almost orthodox to use reward-punishment systems as the primary method of behavior control with challenging students. There is also dissonance between methods used to *manage* behavior and those that foster lasting behavior *change*. Too often, prevailing systems of management work against positive change.[41]

Karen Vander Ven has been a leading critic of superficial behavior management approaches, particularly mechanical point and level systems. This is an example of how such a system operated in an adolescent treatment program in Ontario, Canada:

> Residents are required to negotiate all aspects of their daily lives. Behaviors are observed, documented and altered through agreed upon/contracted use of reinforcers, which were proposed to bring about changes in problematic behaviors…When a resident chooses to be cooperative, this results in rewards, increased privileges and greater independence. However, poor choices result in consequences, more controls and loss of privileges.[42]

This is certainly not a discussion of *choices* in the sense of personal autonomy. Yet those who implement such models seem oblivious to the coercive nature of such an environment. In fact, the developer of the Ontario program described it in glowing terms like *milieu therapy, healing through meaning, enhanced communication,* and *positive peer pressure*. In reality, this is not even good behavior modification since applying reinforcement systems to all youth in a program is like giving identical medical treatments to all patients regardless of their diagnosis.[43]

The popularity of reward-punishment schemes over the last forty years is testament to the fact that these models must be *reinforcing* to the staff even if not to the students. There is no question that social order is essential in any program for youth. But the effect of these models is to create an artificial culture where all interactions are geared around getting goodies rather than making real changes. When applied to a group en masse, these fail to adapt to needs of youth and lean more on punishment than on positive behavior support. This culture of *pointese* contaminates natural social relationships with adults and focuses on maintaining obedience rather than teaching prosocial skills and abilities.[44]

This critique of reward/punishment systems is consistent with research by our late colleague William Wasmund.[45] He evaluated the social climates of four Ohio residential treatment agencies for troubled youth. Two were using peer helping programs and two employed more typical behavior modification approaches. Students from the peer group programs reported greater satisfaction with their social climates. They rated their environments as more characterized by support, involvement, and freedom for expression of feelings.

Particularly intriguing was the dichotomy between perspectives of adult and youth in the different programs. The data suggest that adult-dominated strategies give rise to two opposing cultures: controlling adults and counter-controlling youth. As control-oriented adults manage behavior, they genuinely believe they are creating an orderly environment. However, students in their programs perceive a very different culture, one characterized by more chaos and disorganization. In contrast, students in the peer helping program reported less staff control but more order and organization than in non-peer programs. They also believed their treatment program was enabling them to address their problems and make positive changes.

Jack Howell who has been a leader in adventure education describes this dilemma succinctly:

The reflexive reaction of adults who are used to being in charge
is to squeeze harder when their charges begin to push the
boundaries…Teenagers sense instinctively that they are ready
for a gradual increase of freedom, autonomy, and responsibility.
Adults have to be hit over the head with the same realization.[46]

Pain-Based Behavior

Children who have difficulty controlling their turbulent emotions display pain-
based behavior, which in turn evokes pain-based discipline. Recent research
shows that a host of emotional and behavioral problems in children result from
complex trauma in their lives. Young children totally rely on the caregivers for
safety and to manage their emotions. But abuse, neglect, violence, and loss
disrupt secure bonds and leave fear and other emotions wildly unregulated.

The combination of terror and utter helplessness defines trauma.
Traumatic events become deeply imbedded in emotional memory and may
slow brain maturation according to psychiatrist Bruce Perry.[47] Such children may
become fixed on self-defeating styles of coping behavior. Bessel van der Kolk
found that the prevailing diagnostic category of Post Traumatic Stress Disorder
(PTSD) doesn't fit traumatized children whose core problem is a lack of self
regulation.[48] They may show a range of other symptoms including anxiety, guilt,
depression, oppositional or conduct problems, attention deficits, and phobias.

Children who have been betrayed or hurt become highly alert to cues
of danger and rejection, and inadvertently re-enact past pain. They develop
patterns of thinking distortions including self blame and a sense of worthless-
ness. Those who act out their pain often evoke more pain in the form of
pain-based discipline. The word punishment comes from the Latin *poena*
which means pain. Punishment may have intended effects with emotionally
stable youngsters, who, of course are the ones who need it least. But it
backfires wildly with traumatized youth, reactivating violent bursts of emotion
and breaking fragile bonds with adults. Promising approaches entail corrective

relationships and the opportunity to explore and reframe past pain in safe environments where children heal, learn, and grow.

Joshua: A Lost Cause

At the moment in his life when Joshua thought he was worthless and discarded, a caring attorney kindled new hope.

My name is Joshua DeLeeuw and I was a lost cause. I was born in Los Angeles to a drug addicted, wife-beating father and a mother trying desperately to escape the demons created by my father. But drugs and alcohol never cure the pain. I was taken away from my mother when I was six years old. By then the state had already accumulated a rather large file with my name on it: problems with attention in school, ripping my teeth out in class and smearing blood on the desk, playing mommy and daddy at school with other kids. I was illustrating all the classic signs of an extremely traumatized child.

I would spend the next years of my life in and out of treatment centers, mental institutions, residential treatment centers, foster homes, one failed placement after another. I was diagnosed with PTSD, ADHD, Conduct Disorder, Bi-Polar I disorder, and polysubstance abuse. All I needed was a consistent base, but no one could withstand the tests my little, wounded soul could conjure up. Every placement failed me, moved me on, kept pushing me into progressively less effective programs until the State of Oregon threw in the towel and quit filing run reports and left me to my own devices.

The only place I had ever felt accepted was on the streets with a family of rejects just like me. When I was 16 years old, the District Attorney called me a *lost cause*. I was devastated. My whole life, I had been waiting for someone to convince me that the tragedies that had infected my life were not my fault, that I could be loved.

Something else happened to me the day they put me in the lost cause file. My public defense lawyer saw something else in me. She saw a little boy who really just wanted to belong, to be a free spirit who could do anything he put his mind to. She saw a young man who had endured extreme pain, endless torture, and had no love for his entire life; all he needed was someone to believe in him. On that day, she decided to invest her spirit, her compassion, and her heart into this case file named Joshua DeLeeuw. After the trial, she put away my case file and pulled out her rolodex and put my name in it. Not my number, or my file, but my name.

She visited me in the courthouse visiting room after my sentence was given to me. I was crying and angry. I didn't care anymore. I decided if I was a bad seed, a lost cause, a reject, then I would be the best. She wouldn't let me do it. She insisted that I could do something else with my life. It's funny how certain moments of our lives become the epiphanies of our lifetime.

I got put into an intense treatment program. I wrote about all of my worst experiences in poems, short stories, and memoirs. I used creative arts to express feelings I never expressed because they only caused me pain. I started to realize that my pain could be my strength, that I could take all the terrible experiences in my life and explain them through my art. I had to decide to change, but I would never have believed in myself if someone else didn't show me there was something inside me besides pain and bitterness. I graduated at the top of my class with a degree in psychology and have run a non-profit creative arts program for at-risk youth.

Our children need people to believe in them. Extremely traumatized children are constantly shifted and discarded through the system without ever having any stability. These children need people to invest in them for the rest of their lives.[49]

[1] Angelou, 1998.

[2] Brown, 1991.

[3] Murray, 1938.

[4] Konner, 2002.

[5] Brokenleg, Van Bockern, & Brendtro, 1991.

[6] Hewlett, 1992, p. 34.

[7] Deci, 1995.

[8] Benson, Williams, & Johnson, 1987.

[9] Csikszentmihalyi & Larson, 1987.

[10] Csikszentmihalyi, Rathunde, & Whalen, 1993.

[11] Givens, 2008. This is a very useful compendium of nonverbal cues tied to dominance, submission, and scores of other categories of behavior.

[12] Lewis, Amini, & Lannon, 2000.

[13] Givens, 2008.

[14] Givens, 2008.

[15] Konner, 2002.

[16] Peterson, Maier, & Seligman, 1993.

[17] Sternberg & Kolligan, 1990a.

[18] Sternberg & Kolligan, 1990b.

[19] Bandura, 1994.

[20] Bandura, 1990, p. 315.

[21] Bandura , 1990, p. 318.

[22] van der Kolk, McFarlane, & Weisaeth, 2007.

[23] Tileston, 2006.

[24] Bandura, 1990.

[25] Steinberg & Cauffman, 1996.

[26] Redl, 1966.

[27] Taylor, 2002.

[28] Mullin & Hinshaw, 2007.

[29] Jenkins, 1954.

[30] Gold & Osgood, 2002.

[31] Mitchell & McKenzie, 2006.

[32] Ross, 2007.

[33] Konner, 2002.

[34] Fuller, 2003.

[35] Lewis, 2001.

[36] Hyman & Snook, 1999, p. 60.

[37] Sperber & Wilson, 1986.

[38] Shamay-Tsoory, Tomer, & Aharon-Peretz, 2005.

[39] Long & Long, 2001.

[40] Sue, et al., 2007.

[41] Olive, 2008.

[42] Tompkins-Rosenblatt & VanderVen, 2005, p. 2.

[43] Fox, 2001.

[44] Tompkins-Rosenblatt & VanderVen, 2005, p. 2.

[45] Wasmund, 1988.

[46] Howell, 2007, p. 45.

[47] Perry & Szalavitz, 2007.

[48] van der Kolk, 2007.

[49] DeLeeuw, 2006, pp. 5-7.

CHAPTER SEVEN

Moral Maps

There is a vast empirical literature indicating
that empathy facilitates altruistic, helping behavior;
that it fosters warm close personal relationships;
and that it inhibits personal aggression.[1]
- June Price Tangney -

ANTHONY'S SHOES ARE COVERED IN MUD. *He's hot, he's tired – and he's content.*
He can't explain it. That morning, when the counselor announced that they'd all
be going over to a farm near the detention center to help the family clean up
after a recent tornado, he was furious. Are they paying us? No, said the counselor.
This is something we do because they are our neighbors and they need us.

Empathy is the foundation of moral development and prosocial
behavior.[2] The original word began in the German language as *Einfuhlung*
which is literally translated as *feeling into*. Empathy taps the ability of mirror
neurons to display in our own brain the emotions, thoughts, and motives of
another.[3] Empathy allows us to share another's joy and pain and motivates
care and concern.

Psychologists are newcomers to studying virtue which has long been
the domain of philosophers and poets.[4] Walt Whitman painted the power
of empathy in these words: "I do not ask whether my wounded brother suffers.
I will myself be this wounded brother." Researchers have only recently
recognized this most central human drive insures our well-being and survival.
Empathy gives life a sense of purpose beyond self absorption. It is the
foundation of prosocial values and behavior.[5]

Be Fair and Care

Humans have *moral minds,* say researchers in anthropology, psychology, and neuroscience. First, *Nature* builds a universal sense of right or wrong in the human genome. Then, *Nurture* develops – or warps – this natural capacity for virtue.[6]

Be fair and *care for others* are the brain's primary moral scripts. Carol Gilligan[7] calls these principles *justice* and *caring.* Justice demands fairness, that all have equal access to liberties. Caring calls for sharing to help those in need.[8] At the core of both of these principles is empathy. Humans innately are disposed to treat others the way they want to be treated. This, of course, is the Golden Rule, which is universal across all the world's cultures:

> *Buddhism:* Hurt not others in ways that you yourself would find hurtful.
> *Christianity:* Do unto others as you would have them do unto you.
> *Islam:* No one of you is a believer until he desires for his brother that which he desires for himself.
> *Judaism:* What is hateful to you, do not to your fellow men.
> *Taoism:* Regard your neighbor's gain as your own gain and your neighbor's loss as your own loss.

Social rules and moral values have very different functions. Rules are used for group coordination and order. Moral values deal with meatier issues. Rules may serve to create social stability, but only deep moral values enable us to live in communities of respect.

While *care and be fair* are the core messages of our moral mind, they operate under the radar of consciousness. Yet children acquire this moral grammar before age four and, by school age, they have an *inner voice* of moral standards.[9] Unless something has gone wrong, they reject aggression and are deeply committed to cooperation and kindness. Unfortunately, research shows that this early morality erodes in the cultures of depersonalized schools and negative peer groups.[10]

Just as children's brains have brain maps for learning language, they also have maps for an inborn *moral grammar.* Linguist Noam Chomsky proposed that the brain is designed to use natural social interactions to form both language and morality, without any formal instruction. Of course, the nature of our language and our morality varies depending upon our verbal and cultural environments.[11]

Giving is more rewarding than receiving – so say scriptures and neuroscience.[12] Subjects in a National Institute of Health study played a computer game while their brains were scanned.[13] They received frequent cash rewards and could donate some to specific charities. Upon receiving money, the brain's pleasure center lit up with a rush of dopamine. But, giving money away lit up this and other reward circuits as well. According to researchers, the added warm glow of giving results from oxytocin released by generosity.[14]

The moral values we follow depend on the part of the brain involved in making a decision. This has been shown in various experiments where subjects are confronted with a hypothetical moral dilemma. The most famous example is the moral trolley dilemma.[15]

Scenario I: You are standing by railway tracks and see five workers who are not aware that a train is rapidly approaching. You have two choices: a) do nothing and five people die or b) push a switch to divert the train to a side track where only one worker will die. *Nine of ten persons pick killing one to avoid killing five.*

Scenario II: You and a large man are standing on a bridge and see five workers on a track below who are not aware that a train is rapidly approaching. You can: a) do nothing and five people die or b) push the man over the bridge, killing him but stopping the train. *Nine of ten persons refuse to push the man over the bridge to save lives.*

The mathematics is the same so what makes the difference? Brain scans show that in Scenario I, the logical brain is dominant and persons make a calculated, cost-benefit analysis. Their action is depersonalized; simply operating a lever is a routine motor response.

However in Scenario II, the person draws on deep-brain moral programs to make a decision. Humans have innate inhibitions against using their bodily power to hurt an innocent person. Thus they make an intuitive decision to preserve that one life based on "gut feelings."

Altruism

Altruism is empathy in action, helping others in need. Neuroscientist Shelley Taylor[16] shows how the instinct to *tend and befriend* is more central to human nature than selfishness and aggression. Humans are unique in that both genders have the capacity for tending. We also have been caregivers throughout our existence. Ancient skeletal remains show that many people with severe crippling disorders lived long lives because someone was taking care of them.

The classic research on altruism is the Good Samaritan experiment.[17] That study involved a group of seminary students who believed they were late for a scheduled lecture on the parable of the Good Samaritan. When encountering a person in need (actually an actor), they hurried by. This demonstrated that when we are distracted or distressed, we fail to display altruism. If we do not see people's pain, empathy does not have a chance.

Many earlier researchers presumed that superior altruism was associated with lofty levels of cognitive moral development only possessed by a few moral giants. Now a remarkable series of studies show a very different picture. Altruistic behavior is strongly grounded in children from their earliest years.

Even babies prefer Good Samaritans. Yale researchers found that six- to ten-month-old infants prefer helpful to unhelpful toys. In the experiment, infants watched a wooden toy struggle to try to climb an incline. Then a second toy would appear on the scene to help the climber up the hill. In another case, a trouble-making toy would try to push the climber back down the incline. When encouraged to play with the toys, most infants consistently chose the ones that acted nice.[18] Their young brains are designed to seek out those who help and shun those who hinder or hurt.

The little hands of toddlers reach out to help as early as 18 months of age. Scientists at the Max Plank Institute in Germany found that they readily display altruistic behavior when an adult is in need. The experimenter arranged various opportunities for the children to help. For example, when he appeared to accidentally drop a clothespin, every toddler came to his aid, retrieving the object. Attempts to replicate this with mature chimpanzees were much less successful, apparently because they lacked the level of empathy shown by tiny children.[19]

Lewin found that by age eight, children were frequently "dominated by the ideology of generosity."[20] Children were given four good and four not-so-good toys and encouraged to share. Most gave all four of the best ones to peers, keeping the tattered ones themselves. When they were asked which toys they would really like to have, the eight year olds of course said they preferred the good toys. But in spite of these selfish wishes, their actions were dominated by their ideals.

Group belonging seems to automatically prime altruistic behavior. In 1920, social psychologist William McDougal wrote that loyalty towards members of one's group was the principle moralizing force in society.[21] Modern research confirms this view. When we feel we belong to a group, our in-group empathy programs kick in and activate pro-social behavior without any need for external rewards.

Growing up in cultures of disrespect impairs this natural ability of children to show empathy and altruism. Caring is not fashionable among many modern youth. Weakly bonded to family or school, youth form negative youth subcultures and become trapped in self-centered, exploitative lifestyles. The antidote to this cultural narcissism is straight-forward: motivation for helping is rekindled by secure attachments to a group.

Cohesion in a group is the equivalent to trust between individuals.[22] Research in Re-ED programs shows that strongly cohesive groups are powerful agents for positive support and change.[23] Unfortunately, peer cliques and gangs often do a better job of building belonging than adult-operated youth programs.[24]

There is a widespread misperception that *antisocial youth* will not respond to treatment but need controlled environments with consistent rewards and punishments. Nothing in that custodial prescription addresses their most basic need to reciprocate love. Typical punitive sanctions for such young persons only serve to reinforce a cycle of recidivism and disengagement from pro-social roles.[25] On the other hand, persons using touchy-feely approaches will be seen as weak and thus be equally ineffective.

Michigan peer influence studies show that the most effective adults are those who can combine strong accountability for pro-social behavior with strong encouragement and support.[26] We call this "demanding greatness." Contributing to others activates deep empathy programs. Even very troubled individuals are likely to have some intact underlying moral competence which can be the basis for positive development.[27]

Virtue and Vice

Although humans inherit a biological bias that permits them to feel anger, jealousy, selfishness, envy, and to be rude, aggressive, or violent, they inherit an even stronger biological bias for kindness, compassion, cooperation, love, and nurture – especially toward those in need.[28] - Jerome Kagan

The brain is endowed with programs for *virtue*, a word that comes from the Latin *virtus*, meaning strength. As social beings, humans need moral strengths to live successfully in groups.[29] While cultures define the specifics of virtue and vice, the brain already starts with inbuilt standards which are biased in the favor of good over evil.

Morality is defined by our polarized social emotions. We are inspired by some acts but find other behavior reprehensible. Polar emotional reactions of *elevation* and *disgust* send signals from brain to heart and gut. Elevation causes a warm, tingly feeling in the chest. Disgust literally makes us sick to our stomach.[30]

The highest moral virtue is to be of value to others. This is more than an ethical principle, it is mapped in our genes. William Damon describes how the human brain is programmed to provide a burst of *moral elevation* when we act with empathy and benevolence to others. Only a prosocial purpose can provide the lasting inspiration, motivation, and resilience required for a truly meaningful life.[31]

Human brains use complex social emotions to guide our decisions about whether behavior is right or wrong.[32] This is what happens with our thinking and feelings in moral situations:

Blaming or Empathizing. The high speed social brain makes snap judgments about problems involving others and triggers either blame or empathy. Blame is related to emotions like disgust or contempt while empathy is tied to sympathy and compassion. We are more likely to blame others who cause us personal distress, particularly if we do not have a trusting relationship with them. Empathy is more likely when we have a positive connection with persons and are attuned to their pain or need.

Esteeming or Demeaning. We also make warp speed judgments about behavior or personal qualities we find attractive or repulsive. Esteeming is tied to emotions of admiration and gratitude, while demeaning is related to dislike and disinterest. Our life experiences bias us to look for either the positive qualities or flaws in others. Many troubled kids assume the worst about adults – just as adults with pessimistic mindsets also assume the worst about troubled kids.[33] This makes a caustic combination.

Self-Judgments. Humans also have brain programs to judge their own behavior. Self-blame is tied to feelings of embarrassment, guilt, or shame. When we demean ourselves, we feel inadequate and unworthy. When we hold ourselves in esteem, we feel pride. If we are attuned to our own feelings, we are better able to evaluate our role in conflicts with others.

The stories of a culture mark the esteemed moral values as reflected in tales of heroism, kindness, and self-sacrifice. Just hearing such stories can create the same patterns in the brain as experiencing or seeing the act itself.

The most inspiring human actions are those related to compassionate or courageous behavior. Observing these moral actions creates heartfelt, visceral feelings and motivates persons to engage in such behaviors themselves.[34]

Since humans have deep needs for Belonging, Mastery, Independence, and Generosity, our mirror neurons register vicarious satisfaction when we see others meet these needs. Thus we empathize with the joy expressed by family members reunited at an airport, even if we do not know who they are. We are inspired by performances of great athletic or artistic prowess, as if these were our own victories. We resonate with fellow humans who break free from oppression to gain their freedom. And more than all else, our hearts resound to acts of generosity. Of all human interactions, acts of altruism are the single most inspiring and motivating events.[35]

Social institutions also reinforce core values through stories and imagery of noble deeds. What distinguishes outstanding organizations is their saga which binds members in a common purpose. Students, staff, and supporters at Starr Commonwealth are inspired by the story of Floyd Starr and the first boys living in an old barn. Boys Town captured its mission in the image of two homeless boys. The older youth carries a small boy on his back and tells

Father Flanagan: "He's not heavy, he's my brother." The inspiration of that image made Boys Town another beloved charity.

Powerful acts of generosity are reciprocated by powerful feelings of gratitude, a highly prized virtue across faith traditions and cultures. Only recently have researchers begun to study gratitude, a symptom of psychology's tendency to neglect positive emotions and emphasize negative ones.[36]

Gratitude in response to the generosity of others fosters social bonding and a sense of well-being. Norwegian special education pioneer Kris Juul contended that gratitude was more potent than social reinforcement. Social reinforcement conveys the message: *If I am good, I will be loved.* Gratitude taps into a much deeper motive for morality: *I am good because I am loved.*[37]

The most courageous act of giving is forgiving. Both humans and animals have innate motivations towards reconciliation after periods of conflict. These positive moral emotions often do battle with hatred and vengeance. Children who have been deeply hurt by trauma need to find some way to leave it behind. Persons who have been victimized by crime also need to be able to heal. In Nelson Mandela's words, hatred is like drinking poison and hoping your enemy will die.

Forgiveness frees persons from being prisoners of past pain. Such restorative practices offer a positive alternative to cultures of payback and retribution.[38] A most inspiring example is our colleague Azim Khamisa whose only son was delivering pizza when murdered by a fourteen-year-old gang wannabee. That youth was sentenced to spend much of his life in a California prison. Azim found a common bond with the grandfather of his son's murderer, for they had both lost their boys. Today they work in schools and communities to bring the message of forgiveness to thousands of students. Their mission is to break the cycle of violence and help youth plant seeds of hope in their future.[39]

Hooked on Helping

To create positive school cultures, we need to do more than stomp out bullying and lock out violence. John Hoover, a leading researcher on bullying, calls for a deeper look at the moral and spiritual issues about the worth of all individuals and how they should be treated.[40] This requires a transformation of both cultures and individuals so that hostility and harassment is replaced by concern and helping.[41]

The most powerful way to build prosocial behavior and values is to surround young persons with caring adults and peers. But this poses a particular challenge in peer groups of tough kids who feel obliged to front their hard exterior to one another. Further, adults who are afraid of youth or preoccupied with behavioral coercion will never inspire self-absorbed youth to positive purpose and greatness.

Troubled children do not learn to care about others simply by being exposed to caring adults. Nor can we develop a formal curriculum for caring by breaking it into skills like we might teach an arithmetic lesson. Children must believe they are making some genuine contribution if they are to feel good about themselves. Unfortunately many youth initially resist being altruistic or helpful. "Why should I care? I'll take care of myself." They may even see hurting behavior as fashionable while helping others or being "nice" is a sign of weakness.

How can young people who have experienced major difficulties in their lives make significant contributions to others? At the most immediate level, we create a group culture where young people respond with empathy and concern toward one another. Then we expand and generalize this by involving groups of young people in broader service to the community. Such projects should seem challenging and appeal to their strengths, e.g., "this will be a tough job" rather than "this will be easy." It is preferable to stress what they can do for others rather than emphasize the personal gains they will achieve. Helping projects should be exciting and spontaneous rather than regimented and highly adult directed.

Peer helping programs should teach youth to show concern to all persons, not just one's friends. Groups overcome reticence about helping strangers through positive experiences with young children or the elderly. In time, youth learn to take pride in reaching out to those whom most might find unattractive and unworthy. In thousands of service projects over recent decades, our students have made direct impact on others in need. This may be as mundane as serving in soup kitchens or as dramatic as helping residents of a town devastated by a tornado. Students from Youth Off The Streets in Australia even travel to third world countries to rescue children who are living in garbage dumps. Such experiences provide the ultimate proof of one's own worth, being of value to others.

Youth who have been seen as societal liabilities can be transformed into assets as they become hooked on helping. But the goal should always be on how one can improve the lives of those being served, not of those doing the service. Otherwise, concludes Martin Buber, those entering into helping to satisfy their own needs are condemned to a relationship that will never be complete.[42]

Providing the opportunity for a positive adult and peer bond will evoke prosocial behavior from most youth. But highly traumatized or violentized youth harbor deep-seated pain and delinquent values that initially resist change. They are wary of trusting relationships and have patterns of self-centered thinking which override empathy and silence the voice of conscience. This requires a concerted intervention to reverse negative group cultures, engage youth in helping roles, and teach them new ways of thinking about themselves and their values. These are the goals of Positive Peer Culture programs which the authors and colleagues have been developing for over three decades.[43] In the final chapter of this book, youth from turbulent backgrounds describe how these principles are transforming their lives.

One cannot create positive ecologies for children and youth without a unifying theme of shared beliefs and values.[44] Children and youth thrive in cultures that embody the Circle of Courage values of Belonging, Mastery, Independence, and Generosity. Mortimer Adler[45] notes that most values are culturally relative, but absolute values are tied to universal human needs. Stated in the language of resilience and brain science, all children have innate needs for attachment, achievement, autonomy, and altruism. Meeting these universal needs is the gold standard of effectiveness in education, treatment, and positive youth development.

Becky: We are Good People

After sexual abuse, court problems, school problems, homelessness, and
overwhelming stress, Becky took a cocktail of pills and alcohol: She describes
how youth workers guided her out of her "dark tunnel."

I just wanted to be left alone to die. I just couldn't take anymore.
I just wanted out. I told the doctor and nurse that and they got me locked up
in a psych ward for a month. They gave me heaps of medication to sedate
me through that time. The doctor reckons I am depressed. Wow! Depressed.
I think that's an understatement.

I started hanging out with the kids from town who didn't go to school.
They always accept you for who you are. They are like me. I don't feel like
an X-file. I had a tight little group of people and we are all in the same boat.
That became my family, something I never had before.

I live on my own and want to have school friends stay, and their
parents want to speak to my parents. Well, I don't have anyone because I am
a state ward and these parents think I have done something wrong and
won't let their daughters stay over.

When the school asked for letters for parents/guardians to sign,
I have to get my case officer to sign. I still get upset and cry heaps. We had to
go around the class and tell our story, who we were, brothers, sisters, and
family, what we want to do in the future. I get sad listening to other students
and seeing what they have.

At graduation, I got a certificate in front of all of these people but
there was no one from my family. All the other students have someone
to congratulate them, and this homeless student is standing there on her own.
That's what happened to me.

A lot of people would be surprised how smart these street kids are.
We are good people. Every single kid has dreams of being a lawyer or teacher
or whatever. Given the chance and support, they can achieve their dreams.

I find it hard to trust adults. I feel I always get hurt in the long run. There are not many people in authority who are trustworthy, open, and honest and genuinely care about kids with major problems. You guys hang in there with me no matter what, drinking, suicide, whatever. It's like you walk this dark tunnel with me.

What has helped has been youth workers who have always been there for the crucial times. That's what I want to do. Go to the university and study to be a youth worker to help other kids like me. Maybe those people who make big decisions will read something like this and realize that a kid like me does really try to be good.[46]

[1] Tangney, 2001, p. 133.

[2] Gibbs, 2009.

[3] Sympathy is often used as a synonym for empathy but it usually suggests a somewhat more detached rational concern for the other person's welfare, not direct sharing of feeling (Damon, 1987).

[4] Haidt, 2003, p. 275.

[5] Tangey, 2001, p. 133.

[6] Hauser, 2006.

[7] Gilligan, 1982.

[8] Rawls, 2002.

[9] Tancredi, 2005.

[10] Brendtro, Ness, & Mitchell, 2005.

[11] Hauser, 2006.

[12] Moll et al., 2006.

[13] Functional magnetic resonance showed activity in the VTA (ventral tegmental area) pleasure center and surrounding deep brain regions when monetary awards were given and also when money was given away!

[14] Haidt, 2006.

[15] Radio Lab, 2006.

[16] Taylor, 2002.

[17] Darley & Batson, 1973.

[18] Hamlin, Wynn, & Bloom, 2008.

[19] Warneken & Thomasello, 2006. While mature chimpanzees lacked the empathy shown by tiny children, apes and all kinds of other animals have been immensely helpful and have shown empathy when the need arose, i.e., when more important issues were at stake than a clothespin.

[20] Lewin, 1943/1999, p. 335.

[21] McDougal, 1920.

[22] Yalom, 1995.

[23] Valore, 2007.

[24] Mikulincer, Shaver, Gillath, & Nitzbert, 2005.

[25] Toch & Adams, 2002.

[26] Gold & Osgood, 1992.

[27] Hauser, 2006, p. 241.

[28] Kagan, cited by Goleman, 2006, p. 62.

[29] Tancredi, 2005.

[30] Keyes & Haidt, 2003. These connections use the vagus nerve and other pathways from our social brain.

[31] Damon, 2008, p. 40. The research base for these ideas is reviewed by Jonathan Haidt, 2006.

[32] Hauser, 2006.

[33] Seita & Brendtro, 2005.

[34] Haidt, 2003.

[35] Haidt, 2003.

[36] McCullough, Kilpatrick, Emmons, & Larson, 2001.

[37] Juul, 1981.

[38] Wachtel, 2003.

[39] Khamisa, 2007.

[40] Hoover & Oliver, 2008.

[41] Gibbs, Potter, Goldstein, & Brendtro, 1996.

[42] Buber, 1970.

[43] Vorrath & Brendtro, 1985; Gold & Osgood, 1992; Gibbs, Potter, & Goldstein, 1995; Wasmund & Tate, 2000; Brendtro, Ness, & Mitchell, 2005; Quigley, 2007; Laursen, 2007.

[44] Wolins & Wosner, 1982.

[45] Adler, 1985.

[46] Excerpted from Glasson-Walls, 2004.

CHAPTER EIGHT

Transformation

It's almost like a new you.
Like you just add a whole bunch of stuff to your brain.

- D'Angelo, Starr Student -

In this chapter, we summarize key principles that lead to transformational change in children of challenge. Once again, the standard of consilience guides our search. We tap evidence from bio-social science and deep democratic values that can inform practice and change lives. Our focus will be on four types of transformation:

- Trauma to Trust
- Performing to Learning
- Deficits to Strengths
- Program Centered to Person Centered

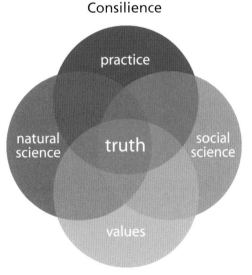

Consilience

practice

natural science

truth

social science

values

Transformation I: *Trauma to Trust*

ALLAN EXPERIENCED REPEATED TRAUMA, FIRST IN A TROUBLED FAMILY AND THEN IN ALTERNATIVE PLACEMENTS. *Shortly before I turned 13, I was removed from my family and placed in private boot camps in California and Idaho. I guess my brain blocks the bad stuff that happened to me. I put up a wall that is so strong, not even I can take it down. I refused to talk to counselors so they decided to send me to a private residential treatment center in Maine. I hated this place and they hated me. Kids who did something bad were sent to "The Corner" to sit all day. Then during the general meeting, the other kids were required to "confront" the person who had problems. They would surround you, yell, scream, and swear. If this didn't work, the group would restrain you on the floor. If the kids couldn't handle you, staff would use plastic ties on wrists and ankles. I hated being restrained and kept fighting them. I am still careful about whom I trust.*

PRINCIPLE 1: *When a young person shows pain-based behavior, administering more pain only deepens the individual's distress.*

Clinical and brain studies indicate that troubled children react to distressing life circumstances with "pain-based behavior."[1] Allan was a traumatized youngster whose deep personal pain was met by angry confrontation, restraint, isolation, and exclusion. Such strategies are common in practice but have no educational or therapeutic rationale. Ironically, pain-based behavior by children is often met with pain-based discipline by adults.

The most basic ethical principle for helpers is *do no harm*. Yet many who deal with highly challenging youth lack the necessary skills to prevent or manage turbulent behavior. Staff do not consider themselves adequately prepared to handle serious crisis situations.[2] Thus, they react to problems instead of responding to needs. Authoritarian and abusive environments only fuel hostility and disturbance.[3]

The personality and private logic of every child is shaped by a lifetime of positive and negative experiences. Jasmine, a homeless student who attended an alternative school in Australia explains:

> A counselor asked me to write out all the good things that happened to me as a child and all the bad things. I started crying because I could not think of one good thing.[4]

Contrast Jasmine's life with that of children from Highland Peru whom we met in Chapter 2. They are immersed in a culture of respect and protected from serious threat and harm. But in modern culture, our most needy children are those least likely to feel safe and secure.

A growing body of research makes it apparent that most children showing pain-based behavior are reacting to relational trauma. The early onset and persistent problems of these children present huge challenges to families, schools, and communities. While effective interventions are available, current approaches have not yet incorporated this new science and clinical expertise into practice.

PRINCIPLE 2: *Many children with troubled behavior have experienced developmental trauma in their early relationships.*

Abuse, neglect, violence, and disruption of secure bonds evoke terror and utter helplessness in children who totally rely on adults to calm their emotions. Only as their brains mirror comforting caregivers can children gradually learn to calm themselves. But traumatized children have not yet developed such emotional self-regulation. They experience pervasive distress shown by anxiety, fear, rage, guilt, depression, attention deficits, impulsivity, explosiveness, oppositional behavior, and conduct problems. They can be diagnosed with every disorder in the book, but this only focuses on the wrong question. As Sandra Bloom says, it is not *what's wrong with you?* but *what has happened to you?*[5]

The most destructive abuse comes not from stranger danger but from the very individuals children have learned to love. No brain programs exist to deal with the terror of abuse from a trusted person. Typically, traumatized children blame themselves for their mistreatment:

> I have been raped, beaten, and humiliated since I was a little boy. Even my priest did it to me. This doesn't happen to everyone – it's got to be something wrong with me.[6]

Bloom describes how families, teachers, foster parents, and treatment staff all can create a sanctuary, a safe environment where children can heal.[7]

PRINCIPLE 3: *All who deal with traumatized children can play important roles in restoring trust and security by helping to create a sanctuary for healing.*

Restorative relationships offer the opportunity to revisit and reframe past pain in safe environments.[8] Psychiatrist Bruce Perry notes that children who have been damaged by relationships need healing communities that build trust and confidence through secure connections of love.[9] Psychologist William Steele has developed curriculums for training adults to reconnect and build a deep-brain sense of safety and security. Helpers must move beyond traditional clinical roles and seek to understand how trauma is seen in the mind of a young person.[10] Howard Bath of Australia calls on all who care for emotionally wounded children to help them gain safety, connections, and self-regulation.[11]

Children of trauma replay their pain with new actors. Helpers need skills to avoid being drawn into conflict cycles marked by power struggles, counter aggression, and avoidance. Nor can they indulge or enable the child in a role as helpless victim. Instead, these children need adults who will walk with them through the storms of life until they break free of the pain of the past.

PRINCIPLE 4: *Negative peer associations can be transformed into positive peer influence.*

Schools and group programs that put troubled students together can easily deteriorate into a *Lord of the Flies* subculture. One of the first to document this was sociologist Howard Polsky who lived for eight months in a residential group of delinquent boys. Beneath the treatment veneer of the program was an underground culture of peer bullying and rule breaking. Polsky called for research on new approaches to counter this negative peer influence.[12]

Two polarized methods emerged to tap the power of peer influence: the *hot seat* versus the *helping circle*. The first gives youth a license for peer pressure, the second for peer concern. Using youth to discipline rule-breakers has long been a popular panacea in coercive environments since it requires little staff training – just turn peers loose on troublemakers. But creating a climate of peer concern takes careful staff training and a commitment to values of respect.

Forty years after his original research, Polsky updated his views of peer influence.[13] He had initially been impressed with the "normative culture" model developed by Sam Ferrianola who headed Glen Mills Schools in Pennsylvania for three decades. Intense confrontation by staff and peers was used with those who did not conform to norms.[14] The master norm was that all staff and students must confront any norm violator. *"If not, the non-confronter is confronted for not confronting."*[15]

Absolutely no dissent was tolerated as this was another infraction called "going out of process." As former students explain, this means that any attempt to complain to parents, court officials, or other outsiders about treatment at the school led to severe punishment.[16]

Polsky acknowledged that although some youth can adapt to such confrontational systems, "a massive, suffocating thought-police system comprised of both staff and student look-alikes has been created."[17] Enforcing "norms" became a closed cult system which overpowered and ostracized those who do not submit to standards. Such approaches violate core values of creating democratic communities which respect the autonomy of all students.

Youth Today described a Maryland academy for delinquents using the "normative culture" model which was closed after the death of a student in a four-hour physical restraint.[18] Staff training prescribed that no violation of "norms" was to be ignored. Tools of behavior control were "thousands" of confrontations each day by staff and peers.[19] True positive cultures are not based on thousands of acts of confrontation but thousands of acts of helping. Youth are not engaged as enforcers but as peer helpers.[20]

Transformation II: *Performing to Learning*

The broad effects which can be obtained by punishment in man and beast
are the increase of fear and sharpening the sense of cunning....
punishment tames but does not make one better.[21]
- Friedrich Wilhelm Nietzsche -

The purpose of learning is to create better human beings. The brain is a deep depository of knowledge to help us to survive and thrive. But empty experiences soon fade from memory.[22] In the end, we are all shaped by memories and the meanings we attach to these.

PRINCIPLE 5: *The events stored in a child's memory – and how the child interprets these – set the course of development.*

Synapses hold our fondest and most fearsome memories, says Nobel Prize winner Eric Kandel.[23] He demonstrated how brain cells convert fleeting short-term memory into enduring pathways in the brain. The decision on whether to STORE or IGNORE an experience is made by two dueling brain chemicals that either enhance or suppress memory:

1. STORE chemicals (CREB-1) instruct the brain to create long-term memories by activating genes so neurons can grow new connections.[24]
2. IGNORE chemicals (CREB-2) keep the brain from constantly redesigning itself, blocking formation of permanent memories except when necessary.

STORE chemicals horde memories, but IGNORE chemicals keep the brain from becoming buried by mountains of trivia. This same process applies to conscious (explicit) memories as well as to unconscious (implicit) emotional memories.

Long-term learning blazes new trails in the brain. Short-term learning only follows the well-worn ruts of the past. When an experience produces short-term learning, there is merely a transmission of chemicals along established brain circuits. But with long-term learning, the brain lays down fresh pathways to deal with challenging problems. The sum of these connections forms our personality; our brains become who we are.[25]

PRINCIPLE 6: *Emotionally charged events are potent learning opportunities. Repeated experiences or messages also can create deep brain learning.*

What information goes into deep storage in our brains? Neurons have two in-built standards for deciding what should be archived in long-term memories:

1) **Emotionally-charged experiences** signal to the brain that this positive or negative event is worth noticing and perhaps remembering. But boring, irrelevant information is suppressed. Even if we are forced to learn dull facts, IGNORE chemicals keep telling us these are not worth remembering. Since the brain uses a *store stirring stuff* rule, every crisis situation or pleasurable experience opens a window for learning new coping strategies.

The darkest variety of deep brain learning comes from trauma: painful memories keep intruding into the present. Since repeated activity shapes the brain, chaotic experiences can block normal brain development. But through focused repetition of positive experiences, the brain can be redesigned and healed.[26]

2) **Repeated learning trials** are required in order to STORE information that fails the excitement or novelty test. This is how we drum multiplication tables into our minds. However, most learning trials do not involve conscious memorization but millions of repeated experiences across our life history. The culture of a family, school, peer group, or community is a silent curriculum which can direct the course of development. We are not even consciously aware

of how continual cultural immersion shapes our personality and private logic. As anthropologists say, fish fail to notice the water in which they swim.

This principle is put to use in building cultures of respect through frequent repetition of important ideas and values. Scripts such as *if you're not helping, you are hurting* become so pervasive that they transform values, thinking, and behavior. If youth come with entrenched self-centered attitudes (e.g., *I'll watch out for number one*) these can be respectfully challenged. When delinquent acts are described as cool, they can be relabeled as *immature* or *hurting others*. Delivered with genuine concern, these scripts tap into innate deep brain motivations for belonging and generosity towards others.

Most learning is short term and quickly lost – not necessarily bad since our brains avoid being overloaded with trivial matters. Unfortunately, this aptly describes ho-hum school curriculum and humdrum personal relationships.

PRINCIPLE 7: *Task motivation fosters genuine learning and change. Egoistic motivation causes defensive or deceptive reactions to protect from threat.*[27]

Egoistic motivation results in reactive behaviors to protect against failure. Encountering a problem, youth avoid difficult challenges and display helplessness, avoidance, or resistance. Some cheat to hide inadequacy or build bravado fronts to mask failure and defend their reputations. Motivation to *look good* interferes with learning and growth goals.[28] Superficial performance is exaggerated by high stakes testing and point level behavior modification systems.[29] Such policies actually deepen brain pathways for defensive or deceptive behavior.

In contrast, youth who focus on task goals invest in mastery learning and personal growth. They are not discouraged by errors but use these to design more adaptive responses. They become deeply involved in the challenge at hand and set aside being self-conscious about performance. Positive intrinsic motivation has aptly been called *flow* since one is on a roll searching for creative solutions.[30] The power of flow is seen as students become fully engaged in school, seeking to learn instead of perform. Flow abounds as youth become hooked on helping, putting aside selfish concerns to reach out to a friend in need. In flow, the brain becomes a pro at problem-solving.

PRINCIPLE 8: *Effective programs focus on those factors that have the most clout in producing lasting positive change and development.*

Success with challenging youth requires deep and enduring change, not just surface compliance. Yet that is the standard used in many programs. Recently we heard a new *diagnosis* for disruptive kids: *FTA*. We were told that this acronym stood for *failure to adapt*. Adapting to a program is no proof of its effectiveness.

Many methods vie for the label *evidence based*. Typically this means that technique A won out over technique B at some level better than chance. So what? *Statistical significance* in a research study usually has little to do with *significant life change* in an individual.

In statistical jargon, the important question is the *size of the effect.* Without knowing effect size, we cannot tell if a measurable difference is of any practical difference. It is not hard to design a study to produce some statistically significant finding, however irrelevant. With a large enough sample size, the most minuscule difference rises to *significance*.

A large body of evidence points to a few key variables that have the greatest influence on therapeutic and educational improvement. An important meta-analysis published by the American Psychological Association is summarized in the accompanying circular graph.

Factors Influencing Positive Change

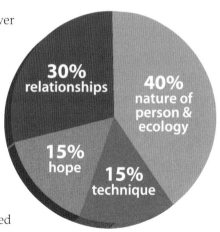

Adapted from *The Heart and Soul of Change.*
Hubble, Duncan, & Miller

The nature of the person and ecology account for 40% of positive gain. Next comes the helping relationship which produces 30% of the effect. Finally, hope and technique each contribute 15% to the outcome.

PRINCIPLE 9: *Powerful interventions build strengths in the person and supports in the ecology.*

Unique personal and environmental characteristics wield the most potent influence. Behavior is a function of a person in an environment.[31] Peter Benson from the Search Institute shows that positive youth development is fostered by internal and external assets.[32]

Internal assets include social competence, commitment to learning, positive self identity, and positive values – similar to Circle of Courage principles of Belonging, Mastery, Independence, and Generosity. Children who develop these assets are on the pathway to resilience. But whatever prevents development of these strengths fuels risk and poor outcomes.

External assets include relationships and opportunities to support youth in meeting growth goals. This applies to all areas of the ecology, including families, schools, peer groups, and community mentors. For example, by strengthening family bonds, we increase external assets for a youth. But professionals who search for strengths in youth often approach families with a deficit mindset. A resilience lens shifts the perspective from viewing families in distress as damaged to seeing them as challenged and capable of healing and growth. Instead of focusing on how families have failed, we redirect our attention to how they can succeed. Rather than giving up on troubled families, we seek to build a partnership to foster growth in young persons and their families.[33]

PRINCIPLE 10: *Success with challenging youth entails disengaging from adversarial encounters and building respectful alliances.*

The helping relationship turns out to be a powerful force for change, accounting for 30% of positive outcome. This also applies to successful school programs for students at risk.[34] However, many adults do things *to* or *for* youth rather than joining *with* them in an alliance.[35]

The illustrations below compare *The Respectful Alliance* with *The Adversarial Encounter.* These involve competing brain programs for trust and distrust.

The Respectful Alliance

Trust – the youth believes the adult cares, understands, and is able to help.

Cooperation – the youth and adult work together for mutual benefit, e.g., both youth and adult join forces to solve a problem.

Connection – reciprocal harmony and respect characterize the relationship.

The Adversarial Encounter

Distrust – the youth believes the adult won't care, understand, or be able to help.

Discord – the youth and adult don't share goals, e.g., the adult seeks control or change but the youth wants autonomy.

Disconnection – reciprocal conflict and avoidance characterize the relationship.

Distrust is sparked by any sign of threat which arouses the amygdala. But trust is activated by the brain's bonding hormone, oxytocin. When someone observes that another person trusts him or her, oxytocin floods the brain, overriding distrust.[36] Floyd Starr sometimes recruited delinquent teens to serve as his chauffeur to gain their trust. August Aichhorn of Austria would send little thieves out with big bills to purchase something from the market place. One does not have to be that risky, since nonverbal expressions of trust and attraction trigger reciprocal reactions in the other person's brain. But those who fear or dislike youth will not be able to set in motion this dance of trust.

PRINCIPLE 11: *Hope builds spiritual strength and self-efficacy, giving the young person the courage to change.*

Hope and positive expectancy account for 15% of improvement. Any intervention which is seen in a positive light by some persons is likely to produce placebo effects, even if the program is weak or worthless. Hope empowers those who are discouraged or demoralized. Hope builds self-efficacy and counters a sense of futility and helplessness. Hope improves healing: secular researchers have identified prayer and meditation as a contributor to recovery following serious medical crises.[37] Hope is contagious: the positive morale of a group to which one belongs can contribute to resilience.[38]

PRINCIPLE 12: *Specific techniques may have limited impact but should not detract from or undercut broader goals such as building a climate of trust.*

Techniques and specific interventions have a small but limited impact of about 15%, equal to the placebo effect. Although other factors are more important, many researchers aggressively seek to prove the efficacy of technique-based interventions. This is a result of the allegiance they have to a particular model. Unbiased studies often show disappointing results for narrow treatments. Still, some methods do have better results than others.

William Morse always warned that the technique of life space interviews should not overshadow the reality that this was a way of building relationships with children in conflict.[39] Excessive attention to method distracts from other important goals. Therapists who are enthralled with some diagnostic scheme fail to really listen to their clients. Schools obsessed with surveillance strategies to reduce weapons jeopardize a climate of trust.[40]

Many interventions used with youth are borrowed piecemeal from research on other populations, such as therapy with adults. Instead of transplanting narrow strategies, effective interventions are tailored to biological, psychological, and social development in the ecology of childhood.[41]

Techniques are only useful if they support the primary goals of positive development. A prominent example is motivational interviewing, first used in addiction counseling but now applied to a wide range of problems.[42] In the past, if individuals were not motivated to change, the helper would try persuasion or coercion or write them off as resistant. Instead, motivational interviewing mobilizes the person's own values and goals to stimulate a desire to change behavior. This is done by exploring ambivalence rather than trying to impose change. For example, the fun of using drugs might be weighed against the damage this is doing to relationships with the family. While specific techniques are used, this is always in the spirit of building a therapeutic relationship, respecting the person's own autonomy, and helping the person clarify problems and develop goals for change.

Transformation III: *Deficits to Strengths*

PRINCIPLE 13: *Reclaiming programs have a unifying theme based on values that address the most basic needs of children.*

Reclaiming interventions can set youth on new pathways to responsibility. When we arm them with the skills needed to manage life's problems, students become their own change agents. Then the bigger challenge becomes how to ensure that these gains continue after youth transition out of school or treatment. The question is not why a youth fails to maintain positive behavior but how we develop natural settings to support the desired behavior.[43]

Children of challenge need many methods for their many needs. Thus successful approaches are likely to be *psychoeducational*, which means they employ a range of strategies drawn from various theory bases.[44] But *try anything eclecticism* is like choosing a pot luck meal while blindfolded. Core values and beliefs need to guide methods and mindsets. A *unifying theme* is the central characteristic of a reclaiming environment, according to Israeli researcher Yochanan Wozner.[45] Without a common outlook, programs deteriorate into conflict and chaos.

PRINCIPLE 14: *The universal growth needs of children and youth are Attachment, Achievement, Autonomy, and Altruism. These are foundations for resilience and positive youth development.*

The brain has inbuilt maps for efficient responses to the common challenges facing humans over their long history.[46] The Circle of Courage values of Belonging, Mastery, Independence, and Generosity match bio-social needs of Attachment, Achievement, Autonomy, and Altruism. The more education matches how the brain is designed, the more efficient and enduring is learning.

To apply the standard of consilience, Circle of Courage principles are compared with other prominent models in the accompanying table. Common threads run through research on self-worth, personality, and resilience.[47] Similar themes are found in key practice philosophies including Invitational Schools, Teaching Families, and Peer Helping models.[48]

Consilience: A Unifying Theme

Cultural Virtues	Biosocial Needs	Brain Programs
Belonging	Attachment	Trust Maps
Mastery	Achievement	Challenge Maps
Independence	Autonomy	Power Maps
Generosity	Altruism	Moral Maps

Self Worth	Personality	Resilience
Significance	Love, Belonging	Social Competence
Competence	Esteem, Recognition	Problem Solving
Power	Self Actualization	Autonomy
Virtue	Self Transcendence	Purpose

Ecological and developmental research shows that problems presented by youth in conflict result from disruption of their most basic needs. When these needs are addressed, children can thrive and grow.

The classic research of the developmental view of childhood behavioral problems is the Minnesota Study of Risk and Adaptation by Sroufe and colleagues.[49] Emotional and behavioral problems result from transactions between the child and the environment. Simply stated, the youth is using maladaptive coping strategies to meet challenging life circumstances without adequate support. This contrasts with the view that problems result from some *deficit* in the child.

PRINCIPLE 15: *Children thrive when their biosocial needs are met in the ecology of family, school, peer group, and community.*

Positive outcomes are not possible in a climate of conflict between youth and adults.[50] How can we create cultures of respect with highly challenging youth? We draw heavily from studies by the Institute of Social Research at the University of Michigan on personality and peer influence with troubled youth.[51] This was the most extensive series of studies ever undertaken with such populations. It involved substantially all of the delinquent youth served in the major public and private residential programs in the State of Michigan including Starr Commonwealth.

The Michigan Peer Influence project was a longitudinal study of 44 self-contained small group programs serving over 400 youth. Researchers examined the nature of youth and the ecology of the treatment programs. While all settings used some form of peer group programs, these differed depending on the dynamics of the staff teams. Findings from this series of studies are highlighted in terms of the universal growth needs of attachment, achievement, autonomy, and altruism.

Attachment

PRINCIPLE 16: *All youth benefit from strong positive attachments to adults and peers. But repairing these bonds is critical for beset children.*

Youth in conflict experience disruptive interpersonal relationships. This is true of all three major patterns of problems first described by Hewitt and Jenkins.[52] These include *withdrawn* youngsters and two types of acting out youth who have been called *buoyant* and *beset*. Buoyant youth may be delinquent due to cultural factors but they are more stable and socially competent. Beset youngsters are highly anxious, depressed, and distrustful of others, a product of traumatic early life experiences.[53] Beset youth are "likely to be at odds with everyone in the environment" and present particular challenges in school or group programs.[54] Beset youth start early on life pathways of problem behavior.

Buoyant youth usually show an adolescence onset of conflict with authority.[55]

Buoyant youth generally have an intact capacity to build relationships with both peers and adults although they often gravitate to delinquent peers. Their delinquency is a performance to gain peer approval. But beset youth are deeply distrustful and are not easily able to get support from others. When they do build trust, this can change the course of subsequent adjustment, enabling them to reach out to positive teachers and caregivers.

Staff teamwork and morale are essential to the development of a positive youth culture. A dysfunctional staff team creates a dysfunctional student group. But youth who admire their staff make more enduring and positive change. Student and staff morale strongly mirror one another.

Achievement

PRINCIPLE 17: *School failure fuels problem behavior and poor life outcomes. But positive bonds to teachers and school achievement provide a powerful force for change, even when other areas of life are problematic.*

School success is elusive among many troubled youth even though they may be of normal or higher ability. School failure is a pervasive predictor of bad outcomes. It erodes self-worth and propels youth to seek social relationships with other marginalized youth. School failure fuels delinquency and impairs employability. However, Gold found that "success at school, even after years of failure, can change the nature of their identities and cause them to abandon delinquent values."[56] With opportunity for success, even youth with disastrous academic histories can develop an interest in school.

Troubled youth have the highest dropout rates of any group of students with disabilities.[57] Each year they fall further behind since their rate of achievement is typically about two-thirds that of average students. Fortunately, positive school environments can create substantive gains with most of these students. Several studies show average achievement gains of 1.5 to 2 years for each year enrolled in a positive learning environment.[58]

School effects alone can be a force for positive change, independent of personality or other problems in the ecology. The two qualities shown by successful teachers with at-risk students are: 1) *They prevent students from failing.* This involves frequent feedback and encouragement and individualizing the curriculum to their needs. 2) *They provide uncommonly warm emotional support.* Hostility to authority is part of the delinquent performance of kids whose self-respect has been denigrated by school failure. The more students come to like teachers, the more interested they become in school and the higher their achievement.

Autonomy

PRINCIPLE 18: *Autonomy entails respecting youth and expecting responsibility. Autonomy strongly predicts positive outcomes, particularly with youth who fight authority and embrace delinquent values.*

Youth at risk typically lack responsibility and self-control. Buoyant youth often use their power to fight adults and draw them into conflict cycles. Beset youngsters have very little sense of personal power or autonomy. Neither can they control emotional impulses. Since secure attachment is a precursor to independence, these youth need trusting bonds in order to develop self-efficacy and self-control. This is a basic principle of work with traumatized youth.

Autonomy does not mean giving youth their way but rather their say. Autonomy and attachment are closely intertwined as youth bond more quickly to adults who respect their dignity. Young people are astutely attuned to whether they are treated with respect or in demeaning or patronizing ways.

Youths' perception of autonomy is highly associated with virtually all positive goals, including helping behavior, friendships with youth and staff, and desire to change. Surprisingly, research shows little correlation between youths' view of their autonomy and staff viewpoints. Apparently, adults cannot accurately reflect on whether the way they treat youth is seen as respectful or repressive.[59]

Restrictions on personal freedom are pervasive in settings organized around a curriculum of control. This contradicts a consistent finding that greater autonomy is consistently associated with pro-social outcomes.[60] When adults show respect for the opinions of youth, this directly contributes to positive values and acceptance of educational or treatment goals. In cooperative groups, members share common goals and engage in mutual helping to attain them.[61]

Altruism

PRINCIPLE 19: *Children have an innate capacity to develop pro-social values. But these can only flourish in environments where respect and genuine helping permeate the culture.*

Antisocial values directly contradict motives for altruism. Like besetment, delinquent values and antisocial behavior are also relatively stable traits. Punishment and exclusion only reinforce these patterns. Most youth believe peers are more committed to rule breaking than they are, which motivates them to display toughness. If group norms permit, youth will put down this front. Nine of ten delinquents prefer positive behavior but excessive peer dependency makes them vulnerable to negative peer influence.[62]

For more than a century, scientists have been fascinated with the roots of human compassion.[63] Attachment to individuals or a group increases empathy and helping behavior. This occurs naturally with a family or an in-group but is not automatic with out-group members. However, by providing rich opportunities for helping and creating an ethic of respect, youth develop empathy for others.[64]

Exclusion and rejection block the ability to trust or show compassion.[65] Socially rejected children become extremely wary and are reluctant to risk being hurt again.[66] The more secure young people feel, the more pro-social they become. Altruism is the most direct antidote to self-centered and hurting behavior. Once caring becomes fashionable, youth gain new purpose: they are now of value to someone else.

PRINCIPLE 20: *Enduring change involves building strengths in young persons and then providing them with ongoing support in their natural environment.*

The most effective mentors balance accountability and nurturance. They are equally concerned with responsible behavior and meeting students' needs. Successful staff teams are characterized by cohesion, involvement, belief in program success, and positive expectations about students. They believe that they can have great potential impact on kids whose needs are not being met by others.[67] Taking a positive outlook, they demand greatness instead of obedience.

Across all of the programs in the Michigan Peer Influence Study, "youth were uniformly found to view their living environments as safe."[68] This is noteworthy since many programs which aggregate troubled youth produce negative peer cultures.[69] Peer helping programs attempt to counter this by reinforcing pro-social behavior and accepting responsibility for one's actions.[70]

Safety is a necessary but not sufficient condition for transforming troubled lives. Enduring change addresses primary growth needs.[71] But to maintain these gains, youth need corresponding ecological supports. The pathway to positive change is shown in the accompanying diagram. Positive learning experiences build internal strengths and provide external supports. These are foundations of deep brain learning.

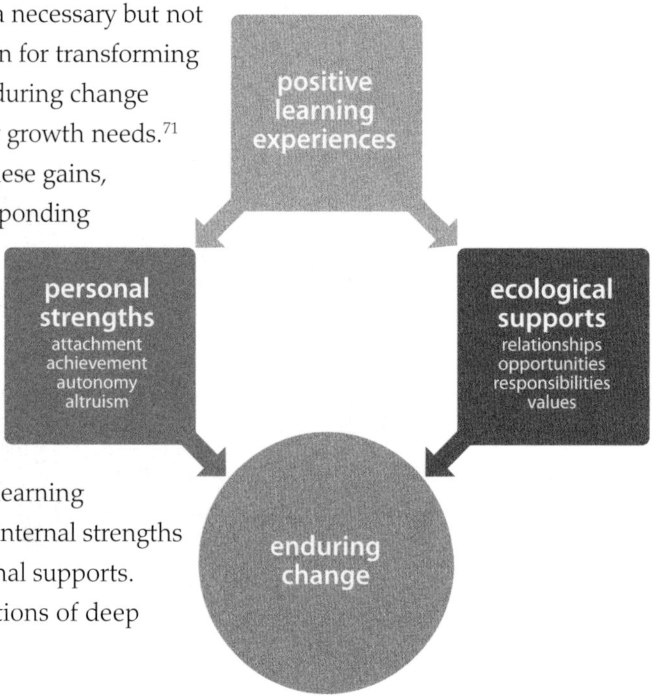

positive learning experiences

personal strengths
attachment
achievement
autonomy
altruism

ecological supports
relationships
opportunities
responsibilities
values

enduring change

Transformation IV:
Program Centered to Person Centered

Programs never change people. People change people.[72]
- John Seita -

As research shows, the largest contribution to positive change comes from the unique person in a unique environment. Thus, the consilience principle requires that youth and families we serve be considered as a key source of knowledge about what they need. Further, assessment must focus on the quality of interpersonal relationships in the culture of the family, school, or organization. These are central tenets of person centered environments.

Voices of Youth

PRINCIPLE 21:
Young people are the ultimate experts in identifying their needs, problems, and potentials.

In this section, students from campuses of Starr Commonwealth and Montcalm Schools in Michigan and Ohio share their personal perspectives

A student from Montcalm School for Girls presents Maya Angelou with a portrait.

on the key principles under-lying positive growth and change.[73]

126

Attachment

- **I didn't want to talk to anyone.** But that just made them want to talk with me more. Before, when I didn't want to talk to counselors, they acted like it was my fault. Here, people could tell I was having feelings but just bottled them up. They showed a lot of respect and love toward me. When I realized I could trust and share, it felt like my shoulders were uplifted.

- **I was always afraid of being teased.** So I just teased people back, like about their clothes. But it's not how you dress, it's how people really feel on the inside. Instead of reading the book cover, if you could just look at the inside, read a couple of pages and really know what somebody's thinking, I guarantee there wouldn't be no teasing. You have to reach out – they won't come tell you they want a relationship because they're scared they're going to be put down. Here people are up-front with you and make you feel accepted. They're confident with themselves and it makes you feel confident, too.

- **When I was new, others made me feel super comfortable.** People really care about you. You find you are not the only person who has problems. If you mess up, nobody jumps on your back. They tell you what's best for you to do and that makes me feel like being honest and trusting. One of my teachers told me that being successful is not an incident, it's a lifestyle.

Achievement

- **I was always afraid of messing up.** When you make mistakes in school, they come down on you which is why I didn't participate. Here if I make mistakes, people help me and teach me how to do it right. Nobody makes bad comments, nobody calls me dumb. If I don't understand, the teacher will pull me aside and say, alright, if you try this, it will produce the right answer, instead of just telling me what I did wrong. My parents can see a difference in me. I think I carry myself in a successful *yes, I'm worth it* way.

- **I didn't want to go to school.** I was lacking in confidence, so I pushed myself away from school. I wanted to learn, but I didn't want to get teased.

This distracted me, and I would start feeling low. Here they have care and concern about you. Now instead of worrying about what other people think about me, what I want is to get my education.

- **We are on a journey through life to learn.** We are in a state of constantly improving ourselves every day. I also have a service-learning project that I do on my own every Saturday where I help tutor little kids. Even though I'm sacrificing some of my time to relax on weekends, I feel good that I'm helping. That's the purpose of my life, to learn, to help, to share knowledge.

Autonomy

- **I used to have trouble sticking up for myself.** I would get mentally and physically abused by peers, but I would keep running back to them because I just wanted friends. Now I am learning to get a more positive image about myself. I am a leader with younger kids as well. I don't talk down to them because I always used to get talked down to in my school. Helping others is very significant in my life; that is basically what I was built for.

- **I used to fight those who were trying to get me to change.** In other schools, they try to get you to do the right thing by making you *afraid of the consequence.* Now I am learning how to figure out on my own to make good decisions because *it is the right thing to do.*

- **I made a big change in my life.** I came from doing drugs, disrespecting my mother and my whole family. It wasn't that I had to change. You've got to make up your own mind that you're willing to change; otherwise you are just putting up a front. So I am excited that I made a decision to make this big change. It's just like unbelievable. I thought I couldn't do it at first because of all of my problems, but it happened.

Altruism

- **Helping is a very complicated process.** If you can help persons before they get mad, they are more apt to listen to you. But when they are angry, they won't listen because they have these other things going through their head, so they start disrespecting others. Basically you set the pace and calm them down. It is hard to help people who are being disrespectful. You might think they don't want your help or need you, like they are just cruel and cold-hearted. In reality, people really want to help each other, but it is just that they are trying to hide their feelings. You can't just give up on people that easily.

- **We do service-learning projects with the elderly.** Some are not physically able to get their groceries up to their apartments, so we help them and talk with them when they are lonely, maybe even play a couple of games with them. Here is a complete stranger who you don't even know and you just help them out and become friends. Before I got here, I never knew how to build a healthy and positive relationship. I took from the community and now it makes me feel better that I'm giving back to the community.

Pathways to Potential

PRINCIPLE 22: *Genuine transformation results in deep change in values, beliefs, and behavior.*

- **When I first got here I was a negative influence.** I thought people were meant to be used to my advantage. But peers and staff started teaching me that it makes you feel better to help others. I began participating and it made me want to help more consistently. I started looking down at my thinking and looking at my heart and tried to find the real love for people. I pushed it away so long it seemed like I didn't have it any more. But it's still there, you're just hiding it.

- **I was locked up a few times in the past.** In other places, they take away points but they never take time to talk with you. I never got help so I would just go truant. When I was sent here, I was roasting people, trying to make them feel bad because I felt bad about myself. If a staff or a group member tried to help me, I would try to hurt them to drive them away from me. I didn't want anyone to get inside my feelings. But people here don't give up on you. I would see others doing the same stuff I did and could see they needed help. When I started to help, it made me feel good about myself and good about them. It gives me goose bumps and puts a smile on my face. I would try to hide it because I wouldn't want anybody to see me as a mushy person.

- **I used to feel in a very low position.** I didn't see the point of living, like what is the use of going on? I notice that there is one thing that can really help me get out of depression. It took me a while to learn it, but if you go out of your way to help somebody else, you feel better about yourself.

- **People used to say,** *that boy's bad.* As I thought about it, I can't be too bad because others are always trying to help me. Facing my issues was hard because I didn't know how others were going to respond – were they going to call me names? But I saw others taking risks and they weren't hurt; they were getting help. So I began to express myself and found out it feels a lot better to be open and honest. *If you're not helping, you're hurting.*

Characteristics Youth Desire in Adults

Young persons respect adults who model positive qualities they need for their own growth.

- *Humble.* Some staff members have the attitude: *this guy has a lot of problems and we're going to be the ones to help him.* I think adults need to humble themselves, saying: *We all have a lot of problems.* If we work on the same level, we are going to be successful. It's not *I'm right and you're wrong,* but *let's determine what's right.*

- *Caring* is necessary for both staff and students. If you're caring and respectful, you get a reputation. You may not even work with some kids, but as long as they know that you're caring, they'll show you a bit of respect. Caring staff will probably work here for a long time – probably get addicted to helping the young people who come and go in here!

- *Compassion.* I've asked a couple of staff, "Why do you want to work here?" They usually tell me, "Why not, there is someone in the world who needs help." Some have probably been through the same stuff we have and might have ideas that can help me change my life. I really love how staff can just say *this is how I did it and you can try to do it.* I do it and it works! That makes me feel good about myself and I'm sure it makes them feel good about their job.

- *Honesty,* not holding anything back – the ability to talk about everything in a helpful, respectful way. I may not necessarily agree, but I respect that person and our relationship enough to say *I believe you and I'm going to try this.*

- *Respect.* Group members might not always show staff respect because they might be going through some problem. But staff will always come to that person and talk one-on-one or get the group to help. It's always respect around here and that's what I like. When you first get here, you automatically know it is respect, because staff go out of their way to make you feel better and that's total respect. If I'm struggling, you're going to help me. You can't get it any better.

- *Consistent.* I can name numerous staff on this campus – like my whole team – everything they do is genuine because it's consistent. You can tell the staff really like their jobs because they want to help kids. They are constantly thinking about us – how can I meet her needs, how can this be a better place to make her successful?

Frontiers in Assessment

Principles of consilience are transforming assessment. Urie Bronfenbrenner criticized traditional approaches as *the study of strange behavior in strange situations by strange individuals.*[74] The bioecological model shifts the focus to the natural behavior of individuals in the ecology of family, school, peers, and community. This has led to two new models for assessment: *The Developmental Audit®* is person-centered and taps the perspectives of that individual. *The Environmental Audit* is ecology centered and focuses on perceptions of school or organizational climates.

PRINCIPLE 23: *Assessment is transformed when youth are enlisted in examining their interpersonal relationships, life challenges, and goals for growth.*

The Developmental Audit addresses two key questions:
What has happened to bring this young person to this point in his or her life? Where should we go from here to foster healing, growth, and resilience? The Audit is a bioecological assessment grounded in principles of brain science and positive youth development.[75] It focuses on three areas:

1) *Connections:* scanning the child's ecology to identify relationships which contribute either to support or strain.
2) *Challenges:* tapping the private logic of the youth to clarify resilient and self-defeating patterns of thinking, values, and behavior.
3) *Solutions:* restorative planning with specific interventions to strengthen Attachment, Achievement, Autonomy, and Altruism.

The young person is seen as the primary expert and is enlisted in this process of evaluation and planning for growth. The Audit is also used by staff teams to identify the function of behavior and design positive behavior supports.[76] Audits can be used in brief interventions or expanded into comprehensive assessments of risk and resilience.

Schools, courts, and treatment programs encounter an increasing number of very troubled and troubling children and adolescents who confound all efforts at intervention, producing great financial and human costs.[77] The Developmental Audit is a protocol for planning restorative outcomes with such youth whose destructive behavior or chronic problems put them at risk for punitive interventions such as school exclusion or placement in restrictive settings. The Developmental Audit provides a new resource for strength-based assessment.

PRINCIPLE 24: *Environments and organizations are transformed when all participants join to create cultures of respect.*

The Environmental Audit is designed to survey the climates of organizations with particular attention to perceptions of youth and the adults who serve them. Discounting the opinions of young persons because their behavior is troubled contradicts our core values and compromises our ability to improve organizational effectiveness. Positive climates contribute to growth while negative climates undermine learning and pro-social goals. Changing environments may be the most powerful means of creating transformational change in youth.[78]

Starr Commonwealth has a long history of measuring environments in order to improve program quality. At the most fundamental level, ongoing consumer surveys can be used to determine level of satisfaction. For example, a survey of Starr's Maple Village Campus showed these levels of consumer satisfaction on questions from a Likert rating scale completed by parents and referral agency staff:

1. Satisfied with how staff kept you informed about your youth. 95%
2. Satisfied with the educational progress of your youth. 97%
3. Satisfied with the amount of change in the youth's behavior. 90%
4. Satisfied that there were no instances of mistreatment by staff. 97%
5. Satisfied that there were no instances of mistreatment by peers. 91%

Evaluation requires the consilience of multiple measures and viewpoints. Consumer surveys can point to broad areas of problems and successes. Qualitative research can gather suggestions for program improvement, particularly by following up on consumer concerns. Other routinely gathered data includes school achievement scores, behavioral observations, incident reports, and statistics of school holding power – the opposite of dropout rates.

Identifying specific factors that shape organizational climate requires valid instruments specifically designed to gather this data. Rudolf Moos of Stanford University has been a pioneer in the scientific evaluation of climates in schools and treatment organizations.[79] A climate is defined as a relatively stable set of social perceptions by participants in a particular environment. Across many types of settings, the key climate factors are relationships, growth goals, and a coherent system.

Ironically, while many talk about the importance of building positive climates or cultures in organizations, few actually measure progress towards that goal. Starr Commonwealth has been formally evaluating its education and treatment climate since this assessment technology emerged. More recently, Starr and a national network of strength-based programs for youth developed a standardized instrument for surveying such environments.[80] Both students and staff anonymously complete environmental surveys on a regular basis. Results track climates in individual programs which can also be compared to the national standardization sample.

Based on a factor analysis of items in the survey, eight variables shape the development of positive climates. Each is stated with sample descriptors. The first two highlight problems that produce cultures of discord. The other six form the foundation for creating cultures of respect.[81]

Intimidation (eliminate)

Students in the group pick on other students.
Students in the group are afraid of each other.

Counterculture (eliminate)

Students keep their problems secret from the group.
The group makes decisions only to look good for the staff.

Treatment Effectiveness

Group meetings help students.
Students are learning to solve their problems.

Communication

Staff listen to what students say.
Students can openly express personal feelings to staff.

Family Values

Staff think that families are important.

Staff try to improve students' family situations.

Staff Involvement

Staff are involved with students in activities.

Staff make schoolwork interesting.

Staff Effectiveness

Staff know what they are doing.

Staff see problems as opportunities to help students.

Student-Staff Relationships

Staff try to get to know students personally.

Staff respect students.

PRINCIPLE 25: *Building pathways to potential requires multiple perspectives, none more important than a deep understanding of the young person in his or her ecology.*

Consilience is the new standard for effective practice. Knowledge from the natural and social sciences is joined with practice wisdom and democratic values to address the core needs of children and youth. But the greatest contribution to success comes not from any external theory or viewpoint. Instead, factors unique to the individual in the specific environment have the largest effect on life outcomes. A person-centered philosophy keeps the young person at the center of the search for truth.

practice

natural science

social science

values

135

[1] Anglin, 2002.

[2] Dawson, 2003.

[3] Morse, 2008.

[4] Glasson-Walls, 2004.

[5] Bloom, 1997, p. 191.

[6] Bloom, 1997, p. 71.

[7] Bloom, 1997.

[8] van der Kolk, 2007.

[9] Perry & Szalavitz, 2006.

[10] Steele, 2008.

[11] Bath, 2008.

[12] Polsky, 1962.

[13] Polsky & Berger, 2002.

[14] Grissom & Dubnov, 1989.
The authors list hundreds of unwritten norms which are enforced by seven levels of confrontation from peer reminders to physical restraint.

[15] Polsky & Berger, 2002, p. 47.

[16] From an on-going blog with hundreds of entries attacking or defending the methods of Glen Mills Schools. www.topix.com/forum/city/west-chester-pa

[17] Polsky & Berger, 2002, p. 48.

[18] Meyers, 2007.

[19] Myers, 2007, p. 21.

[20] Tate & Wasmund, 2000.

[21] Nietzsche, 1887.

[22] Neath & Surprenant, 2003.

[23] Kandel, 2006. Learning occurs at the level of an individual neuron, and the human brain with its 100 billion neurons is too complex to track isolated memories. However, neurons operate the same in all organisms, so Eric Kandel was able to study learning in a sea snail, Aplysia, which has about 20,000 jumbo sized neurons that can be easily observed. He trained the snail to react to an aversive stimuli, such as a shock to the tail. A single isolated shock created a short-term memory lasting minutes. But a series of four or five shocks created a long-term memory.

[24] Gazzaniga, 2008. The nucleus of each neuron includes chromosomes carrying inherited characteristics. A chromosome consists of proteins and DNA which give genetic instructions. A gene occupies a specific location on a chromosome, and many are related to brain function. These genes may be activated by experience as CREB proteins instruct them to build new brain pathways. CREB is an acronym for cyclic AMP response element-binding protein.

[25] LeDoux, 2002.

[26] Perry, 2008.

[27] Dweck, 1986; Nichols, 1984.

[28] Hagen, 2008.

[29] VanderVen, 2009.

[30] Csikszentmihalyi, 1990, 1996.

[31] Bronfenbrenner, 2005.

[32] Benson, 1997.

[33] Walsh, 2006.

[34] Gold, 1995.

[35] Wachtel, 2003; Fulcher & Garfat, 2008.

[36] Zak, 2008.

[37] Peterson, 2008.

[38] Peterson, Park, & Sweeney, 2008.

[39] Morse, 2008.

[40] Lantieri, 2001.

[41] Weisz & Hawley, 2002.

[42] Miller & Rollnick, 1991.

[43] Goldstein & Martens, 2000.

[44] Brendtro & Van Bockern, 1998.

[45] Wozner, 1982.

[46] Gazzaniga, 2008.

[47] Coopersmith, 1967; Maslow, 1970 (see Koltko-Rivera, 2006); Benard, 2004.

[48] Purkey, 1970; Peter, 1999; Gold & Osgood, 1995.

[49] Sroufe et al., 2005.

[50] Osgood, Gruber, Archer, & Newcomb, 1985.

[51] Gold & Osgood, 1992.

[52] Hewitt and Jenkins (1946) identified three types of troubled youth whom they labeled as socialized delinquents, unsocialized delinquents, and a third pattern of anxious withdrawn children. While withdrawn children may have other adjustment problems, this personality pattern actually protects them from involvement in acting out antisocial behavior. These patterns were subsequently documented by Herb Quay (1987).

[53] Gold, Mattlin, & Osgood, 1989.

[54] Quay, 1987, p. 121.

[55] Moffitt, 2003.

[56] Gold & Osgood, 1992, p. 210.

[57] Morse, 2008.

[58] Brendtro & Wasmund, 1989.

[59] Wasmund, 1988.

[60] Martin & Osgood, 1987.

[61] Atwood & Osgood, 1987.

[62] Gibbs, Potter, & Goldstein, 1995.

[63] Dugatin, 2006.

[64] Stürmer, Snyder, & Omoto, 2005.

[65] Mikulincer, Shaver, Gillath, & Nitzberg, 2005.

[66] Twenge, Baumeister, DeWall, Ciarocco, & Bartles, 2007.

[67] Gold & Osgood, 1992.

[68] Gold & Osgood, 1992, p. 212.

[69] Dodge, Dishion, & Lansford, 2006.

[70] Osgood & Briddell, 2006.

[71] Quigley, 2004.

[72] As a boy, John Seita was removed from 15 court placements before he was placed at Starr Commonwealth at age 12. He is now a professor of social work and youth development at Michigan State University.

[73] Observations are drawn from interviews with focus groups conducted by Martin Mitchell, Herm McCall, and James Longhurst. These included students enrolled in Starr's court referral programs and those attending Montcalm School for Boys and Montcalm School for Girls.

[74] Bronfenbrenner, 2005.

[75] Brendtro, du Toit, Bath, & Van Bockern, 2007.

[76] Koehler, 2007.

[77] Mitchell, 2003.

[78] Ross, Grenier, & Kros, 2005.

[79] Moos, 1974, 1979.

[80] Treatment Environment Surveys developed at Starr by Mitchell and Ameen (1992) were adapted and standardized on a national sample including 2,131 students and 712 staff (Yang, Davis, Ryan, & Wasmund, 1999). Programs involved in standardizing this instrument were associated with Strength Based Services International.

[81] Starr Commonwealth, 1999.

BIBLIOGRAPHY

Addams, J. (1909). *The spirit of youth and the city streets.* New York: Macmillan.

Adler, A. (1930). *The problem child.* New York: G. P. Putnam's Sons.

Adler, M. (1985). *Ten philosophical mistakes.* New York: Macmillan.

Aichhorn, A. (1935). *Wayward youth.* New York: Viking Press.

Allport, G. (1938). *Explorations in personality.* New York: Oxford Press.

American Psychiatric Association. (1952). *Diagnostic and statistical manual of mental disorders [DSM].* Washington, DC: Author.

Angelou, M. (1998). Cited in J. Braxton (Ed.), *Maya Angelou's I know why the caged bird sings: A casebook* (p.154). New York: Oxford University Press.

Anglin, J. (2002). *Pain, normality, and the struggle for congruence: Re-interpreting residential care for children and youth.* New York: Haworth Press.

APA Presidential Task Force on Evidence-Based Practice. (2006). Evidence-based practice in psychology. *American Psychologist, 61*(4), 271-285.

Arciniega, C. G., Anderson, T. C., Tovar-Blank, Z., & Tracey, T. (2008). Toward a fuller conception of machismo: Development of a traditional machismo and caballerismo scale. *Journal of Counseling Psychology, 55*(1), 19-33.

Ariés, P. (1973). *Centuries of childhood.* Baltimore, MD: Penguin Books.

Athens, L. (1992). *The creation of dangerous violent criminals.* Champaign, IL: University of Illinois Press.

Atwood, R., Gold, M., & Taylor, R. (1989). Two types of delinquents and their institutional adjustment. *Journal of Consulting and Clinical Psychology, 57*(1), 68-75.

Atwood, R., & Osgood, D. W. (1987). Cooperation in group treatment programs for incarcerated adolescents. *Journal of Applied Social Psychology, 17*(11), 969-989.

Bandura, A. (1994). Self-Efficacy. In V. S. Ramachandran (Ed.), *Encyclopedia of Human Behavior* (Vol. 4) (pp. 71-81). New York: Academic Press.

Bandura, A. (1990). Reflections on non ability determinants of competence. In R. Sternberg, & J. Kolligian, Jr., *Competence Considered* (pp. 315-362). New Haven, NJ: Yale University Press.

Bandura, A. (Ed.). (1995). *Self-efficacy in changing societies.* New York: Cambridge University Press.

Bateson, M., Nettle, D., & Roberts, G. (2006). Cues of being watched enhanced cooperation in a real world setting. *Biology Letters.* ISSN: 1744-9561. www.pubs.royalsoc.ac.uk

Bath, H. (2008). Caring for traumatized children. *Reclaiming Children and Youth,* 17(3), 17-21.

Bath, H. (2005). Our amazing brains. *Reclaiming Children and Youth,* 14(3), 146-147.

Baumeister, R. F., & Leary, M. R. (1995). The need to belong: Desire for interpersonal attachments as a fundamental human motivation. *Psychological Bulletin,* 117: 497-529.

Benard, B. (2004). *Resilience: What we have learned.* San Francisco: WestEd.

Benedict, R. (1934 [1959]). *Patterns of culture.* Boston: Houghton Mifflin.

Benson, P. (1997). *All kids are our kids. What communities must do to raise caring and responsible children and adolescents.* San Francisco: Jossey Bass.

Benson, P., Williams, D., & Johnson, A. (1987). *The quicksilver years: The hopes and fears of early adolescence.* San Francisco: Harper and Row.

Bergen, D. (2006). Play. In S. Feinstein (Ed.), *The Praeger Handbook of Learning and the Brain,* Vol. 2 (pp. 378-382). Westport, CT: Praeger Publications.

Berns, G., Cohen, J., & Mintun, M. (1994). Brain regions responsive to novelty in the absence of awareness. *DNA Research* 1: 37.

Blair, J., Mitchell, D., & Blair, K. (2005). *The psychopath: Emotion and the brain.* Malden, MA: Blackwell Publishing Company.

Bloom, S. (1997). *Creating sanctuary: Toward the evolution of sane societies.* New York: Rutledge.

Bolin, I. (2006). *Growing up in a culture of respect: Child rearing in highland Peru.* Austin, TX: University of Texas Press.

Bolin, I. (1998). *Rituals of respect: The secret of survival in the High Peruvian Andes.* Austin, TX: University of Texas Press.

Bower, B. (2007). Consciousness in the raw. *Science News,* 172(11), 170-172.

Bowlby, J. (1969/1982). *Attachment and loss: Vol. 1. Attachment.* New York: Basic Books.

Brendtro, L. (2007). The vision of Urie Bronfenbrenner: Adults who are crazy about kids. *Reclaiming Children and Youth,* 15(3), 162-166.

Brendtro, L. (1985). Synergistic relationships: The powerful "SR" of reeducation. *Milieu Therapy, IV*(1), 3-12.

Brendtro, L., Brokenleg, M., & Van Bockern, S. (2002). *Reclaiming children and youth: Our hope for the future.* Bloomington, IN: Solution Tree.

Brendtro, L., & du Toit, L. (2005). *Response Ability Pathways: Restoring bonds of respect.* Cape Town: Pretext Publishers.

Brendtro, L., du Toit, L., Bath, H., & Van Bockern, S. (2006). Developmental audits with challenging youth. *Reclaiming Children and Youth,* 15(4), 138-146.

Brendtro, L., & Larson, S. (2006). *The resilience revolution.* Bloomington, IN: Solution Tree.

Brendtro, L., & Larson, S. (2000). *Reclaiming our prodigal sons and daughters.* Bloomington, IN: Solution Tree.

Brendtro, L., & Long, N. (2005). Psychoeducation in the life space: Meeting growth needs. *Reclaiming Children and Youth,* 14(3), 157-159.

Brendtro, L., & Longhurst, J. (2006). At-risk behavior. In S. Feinstein (Ed.), *Praeger Handbook of Learning and the Brain. Vol. 1,* (pp. 81-91). Westport, CT: Praeger

Brendtro, L., Ness, A., & Mitchell, M. (2005). *No disposable kids.* Bloomington, IN: Solution Tree.

Brendtro, L., & Shahbazian, M. (2003). Becoming strong at the broken places. *Reclaiming Children and Youth,* 12(1), 9-11.

Brendtro, L., & Van Bockern, S. (1998). Courage for the discouraged: A psychoeducational approach to troubled and troubling youth. In E. Meyen, G. Vergason, & R. Whelan (Eds.), *Educating students with mild disabilities* (pp. 47-70). Denver, CO: Love Publishing Company.

Brendtro, L., & Wasmund, W. (1989). The peer culture model. In R. Lyman, S. Prentice-Dunn, & S. Gable (Eds.), *Residential and inpatient treatment of children and adolescents* (pp. 81-96). New York: Plenum Press.

Brokenleg, M. (1998). Native wisdom on belonging. *Reclaiming Children and Youth,* 7(3), 130-132.

Brokenleg, M., Van Bockern, S., & Brendtro, L. (1999). Raising respectful kids. *Reclaiming Children and Youth,* 8(1), 2-6.

Bronfenbrenner, U. (Ed.). (2005). *Making human beings human: Bioecological perspectives on human development.* Thousand Oaks, CA: Sage Publications.

Bronfenbrenner, U. (1984). The legacy of Nicholas Hobbs: Research on education and human development in the public interest: Part 2. *Peabody Journal of Education,* 61(3), 52-70.

Bronfenbrenner, U. (1977). Toward an experimental ecology of human development. *American Psychologist,* 32, 13-531).

Bronfenbrenner, U. (1976). The experimental ecology of education. *Teachers College Record,* 78(2), 157-204.

Brooks, R. (2007). The search for islands of competence: A metaphor of hope and strength. *Reclaiming Children and Youth,* 16(1), 11-13.

Brown, D. E. (1991). *Human universals.* Boston: McGraw-Hill.

Brühlmeier, A. (1976) *Reflections on the thoughts of Pestalozzi.* Cited in:
The task: Revival of moral life. www.heinrich-pestalozzi.de/en. Downloaded 5/15/08.

Buber, M. (1970). *I and thou.* New York: Charles Scribner and Sons.

Bueb, B. (2006). *Lob der Disziplin.* Berlin: Eine Streitschrift.

California Council on Youth Relations. (2007). *Transition Aged Youth Focus Groups: Youth Voice and the Mental Health Services Act.* Conducted by the California Council on Youth Relations. April-May 2007. Report and recommendations. Report prepared by Patricia Johnson and Perry Jones, California Council on Youth Relations.

Cambone, J. (1994). *Teaching troubled children: A case study of effective classroom practices.* New York: Teachers College, Columbia University.

Candland, D. K. (1995). *Feral children and clever animals: Reflections on human nature.* Cambridge, MA: Oxford University Press.

Carter, C. S. (2007). Neuropeptides and the protective effects of social bonds. In E. Harmon-Jones & P. Winkielman (Eds.), *Social neuroscience: Integrating biological and psychological explanations of social behavior* (pp. 425-437). New York: The Guilford Press.

Carter, C. S. (2003). Developmental consequences of oxytocin. *Physiology & Behavior, 79,* 383-397.

Carter, C. S. (1998). Neuro-endocrin perspectives on social attachment and love. *Psycho-neuro Immunology, 23:* 779-818.

Chambers, J. C. (Ed.). (2002). Enchanted with chemicals. Special issue, *Reclaiming Children and Youth, 11*(3).

Chomsky, N. (1979). *Language and responsibility.* New York: Pantheon.

Choudhury, S., Charman, T., & Blakemore, S. (2008). Development of the teenage brain. *Mind, Brain, and Education, 2*(3), 142-147.

Cleckley, H. (1941). *The mask of sanity.* St. Louis: Mosby.

Cooley, C. H. (1902). *Human nature and the social order.* New York: Scribner's.

Cooper, J. (2007) *Cognitive disonance: 50 years of a classic theory.* London: Sage.

Coopersmith, S. (1967). *The antecedents of self esteem.* San Fransisco: Freeman.

Cozolino, L. (2006). *The neuroscience of human relationships: Attachment and the developing social brain.* New York: W. W. Norton and Company.

Csikszentmihalyi, M., & Larson, R. (1987). Validity and reliability of the experience-sampling method. *Journal of Nervous and Mental Disease, 175,* 526-536.

Csikszentmihalyi, M., Rathunde, K., & Whalen, S. (1993). *Talented teenagers: The roots of success & failure.* Cambridge, UK: Cambridge University Press.

Csikszentmihalyi, M. (1996). *Flow: The psychology of optimal experience.* New York: HarperCollins.

Csikszentmihalyi, M. (1996). *Creativity: Flow and the psychology of discovery and invention.* New York: HarperCollins.

Damasio, A. (2003). *Looking for Spinoza: Joy, sorrow, and the feeling brain.* New York: Harcourt, Inc.

Damasio, A. (1994). *Descartes' error: Emotion, reason, and the human brain.* New York: Avon Books

Damon, W. (1987). The lifelong transformation of moral goals through social influence. In P. B. Baltes & U. M. Staudinger, (1996). *Interactive minds* (pp. 198-220). Cambridge, UK: Cambridge University Press.

Damon, W. (2008). *The path to purpose.* New York: Free Press.

Darley, J. M., & Batson, C. D. (1973). From Jerusalem to Jericho. *Journal of Personality and Social Psychology,* 27: 100-108.

Davis, J. Q. (2006). The legacy of "if someone hits you, you better hit back." *Reclaiming Children and Youth* 15(1), 8-10.

Dawson, G., & Fischer, K. (Eds.). (1994). *Human behavior and the developing brain* (pp. 3-66). New York: The Guilford Press.

Dawson, C. A. (2003). A study of the effectiveness of Life Space Crisis Intervention for students identified with emotional disturbance. *Reclaiming Children and Youth,* 11(4), 223-230.

De Becker, C. (1997). *The gift of fear and other survival signals that protect us from violence.* New York: Bantam Doubleday.

Deci, E. (1995). *Why we do what we do.: The dynamics of personal autonomy.* New York; G. P. Putnam's Sons.

DeLeeuw, J. (2006). The lost cause. *Reclaiming Children and Youth,* 15(1), 5-7.

Descartes, R. (1637). *Discours des la Méthode.*

Dewey, J. (1916). *Democracy and education.* New York: Macmillan.

Dewey, J. (1910). *How we think.* Lexington, MA: D. C. Heath.

Dilulio, J. (1996). *How to stop the coming crime wave.* New York: Manhattan Institute.

Dodge, K., Dishion, T., & Lansford, J. (2006). *Deviant peer influences in programs for youth.* New York: The Guilford Press.

Dodge, K., & Somberg, D. (1987). Hostile attribution biases among aggressive boys are exacerbated under conditions of threat to the self. *Child Development,* 58: 213-234.

Dodge, K., Dishion, T., & Lansford, J. (Eds.) (2006). *Deviant peer influences in programs for youth.* New York: The Guilford Press.

Doidge, N. (2007). *The brain that changes itself.* New York: Viking.

Dugatin, L. (2006). *The altruism equation: Seven scientists search for the origins of goodness.* Princeton, NJ: Princeton University Press.

Dweck, C. (1986). Motivational processes affecting learning. *American Psychologist, 41*(10), 1040-1048.

Ecoff, N., Ekman, P., Mage, J. J., & Frank, M. G. (2000). Lie detection and language loss. *Nature*, 405: 139-141.

Eisler, R. (1987). *The chalice and the blade: Our history, our future.* San Francisco: HarperCollins.

Ekman, P. (2003). *Emotions revealed.* New York: Henry Holt.

Ekman, P. (2001). *Telling lies:* New York: W.W. Norton Company.

Erikson, E. (1977). *Toys and reasons: Stages in the ritualization of experience.* New York: W. W. Norton and Company.

Fine, M. (1991). *Framing dropouts: Notes on the politics of an urban school.* Albany, NY: Albany State University Press.

Foer, J., & Steber, M. (2007). Remember this. *National Geographic, 212*(5), 34-55.

Foltz., R. (2008). Medicating relational trauma in youth. *Reclaiming Children and Youth, 17*(3), 3-8.

Fox, L. (2001). The catastrophe of compliance. *CYC Online,* 31. Available at: www.cyc-net.org/cyc-online/cycol-0801-fox.html

Freado, M., Bussell, D., & McCombie, J. (2005). The inside kid; A little light in a dark, dark night. *Reclaiming Children and Youth, 13*(4), 194-198.

Freud, S. (1895/1954). Project for a scientific psychology. Translated by J. Strachey. In *Standard edition of the complete psychological works of Sigmund Freud, vol 1.* London: Hogarth Press.

Fulcher, L., & Garfat, T. (2008). *Quality care in a family setting.* Cape Town: Pretext Publishers.

Fuller, R. (2006). *All rise: Somebodies, nobodies, and the politics of dignity.* San Francisco: Berrett-Koehler Publsihers.

Fuller, R. (2003). *Somebodies and nobodies: Overcoming the abuse of rank.* Gabriola Island, BC: New Society Publishers.

Furstenberg, F., Jr., Cook, T., Eccles, J., Elder, G., Jr., & Sameroff, A. (1999). *Managing to make it: Urban families and adolescent success.* Chicago: University of Chicago.

Gardner, M., & Steinberg, L. (2005). Peer influence on risk taking, risk preference,
and risky decision making in adolescence and adulthood: An experimental study.
Developmental Psychology, 41, 625-635.

Gazzaniga, M. (2008). *Human: The science behind what makes us unique.* New York: HarperCollins.

Gibbs, J. (2009). *Moral development in reality: Beyond the theories of Kohlberg and Hoffman.*
(2nd ed.). Boston: Allyn & Bacon.

Gibbs, J., Potter, G., DiBiase, A., & Devlin, R. (in press). The EQUIP program – social perspective –
taking for responsible thought and behavior. In B. Glick (Ed.), *Cognitive-behavioral
interventions for at-risk youth* (Vol 2). Kingston, NJ: Civic Research Institute.

Gibbs, J., Potter, G., & Goldstein, A. (1995). *The Equip Program: Teaching youth to think and
act responsibly through a peer-helping approach.* Champaign, IL: Research Press.

Gibbs, J., Potter, G., Goldstein, A., & Brendtro, L. (1996). From harassment to helping with
antisocial youth: The EQUIP program. *Journal of Emotional and Behavioral Problems,* 5(1), 40-46

Gilligan, C. (1982). *In a different voice. Psychological theory and women's development.*
Cambridge, UK: Cambridge University Press.

Givens, D. (2008). *Dictionary of gestures, signs, and body language cues.* Spokane, WA: Center for
Nonverbal Studies. Available on-line at: http://members.aol.com/nonverbal2/index.htm

Glantz, K., & Pearce, J. (1989). *Exiles from Eden.* New York: W. W. Norton and Company.

Glasson-Walls, S. (2004). *Learning to belong: A study of the lived experience of homeless students
in Western Australia.* Master's Thesis. Perth, Australia: Edith Cowan University.

Gluckman, P., & Hanson, M. (2006). *Mismatch: Why our world no longer fits our bodies.*
Oxford, UK: Oxford University Press.

Gogtay, N., Giedd, J., Lusk, L., Hayashi, K., Greenstein, D., Vaitiuzis, D., Nugent, T., Herman, D.,
Clasen, L., Toga, A., Rapoport, J., & Thompson, P. (2004). Dynamic mapping of human cortical
development during childhood through early adulthood. *PNAS*, 101(21), 8174-8179.

Gold, M. (1995). Charting a course: Promise and prospects for alternative schools.
Journal of Emotional and Behavioral Problems, 3(4), 8-11.

Gold, M., Mattlin, J., & Osgood, D. W. (1989). Background characteristics and responses to treatment:
Two types of institutionalized delinquent boys. *Criminal Justice and Behavior,* 16(1), 5-83.

Gold, M., & Osgood, D. W. (1992). *Personality and peer influence in juvenile corrections.*
Westport, CT: Greenwood.

Goldberg, E. (2001). *The executive brain: Frontal lobes and the civilized mind.* New York: Oxford University Press

Goldstein, A. P., & Martens, B. (2000). *Lasting change: Methods for enhancing generalization of gain.* Champaign, IL: Research Press.

Goldstein, A. P., & Glick, B. (1994). *The prosocial gang: Implementing Aggression Replacement Training.* Thousand Oaks, CA: Sage Publications.

Goldstein, A., & Martens, B. (2000). *Lasting change: Methods of enhancing generalization of gain.* Champaign, IL: Research Press.

Goleman, D. (2006). *Social intelligence.* London: Hutchinson.

Grafton, S., Sinnot-Armstrong, W., Gazzaniga, S., & Gazzaniga, M. (Dec. 2006/Jan2007). Brain scans go legal. *Scientific American Mind,* pp. 30-37.

Grandin, T. (1995). *Thinking in pictures.* New York: Doubleday.

Grissom, G., & Dubnov, W. (1989). *Without locks and bars: Reforming our reform schools.* New York: Praeger.

Hagen, A. (2008). *Learning a lot vs. looking good: A source of anxiety for students.* The Professional & Organizational Development Network. http:// faculty.valenciacc.edu/development2/curriculumSecure/active/learning_a_lot.htm. downloaded 9/29/08.

Haidt, J. (2006). *The happiness hypothesis.* New York: Free Press.

Haidt, J. (2003). Elevation and the positive psychology of morality. In C. L. Keyes & J. Haidt (Eds.), *Flourishing: Positive psychology and the life well-lived* (pp. 275-289). Washington, DC: American Psychological Association.

Hamlin, J., Wynn, K., & Bloom, P. (2008). Social evaluation by preverbal infants. *Pediatric Research, 63*(3), 219.

Harmon-Jones, E. (2007). Asymmetrical frontal cortical activity, affective valence, and motivational direction. In E. Harmon-Jones & P. Winkielman (Eds.), *Social neuroscience: Integrating biological and psychological explanations of social behavior* (pp. 137-156). New York: The Guilford Press.

Hauser, M. (2006). *Moral minds: How nature designed our universal sense of right and wrong.* New York: HarperCollins.

Hazm, A. (1064/1963). *A philosophy of character and conduct.* Circa 1064. Cited in K. Menninger, (1963), *The vital balance: The life process in mental health and illness.* New York: Viking Press.

Head, R. (1996). Remembering Brian. *Reclaiming Children and Youth, 5*(1), 6-9.

Hebb, D. O. (1949). *The organization of behavior: A neuropsychological theory.*
New York: John Wiley & Sons.

Heider, F. (1958). *The psychology of interpersonal relations.* New York: Wiley.

Hewitt, L. E., & Jenkins, R. L. (1946). *Fundamental patterns of maladjustment: The dynamics of their origin.* Ann Arbor, MI: Michigan Child Guidance Institute.

Hewlett, B. (1992). *Intimate fathers.* Ann Arbor: University of Michigan Press.

Hobbs, N. (2007). The art of getting into trouble. In R. Cantrell & M. Cantrell (Eds.), *Helping troubled children and youth* (p. 136). Memphis, TN: American Re-Education Association.

Hobbs, N. (1982). *The troubled and troubling child.* San Francisco: Jossey-Bass.

Hofer, M. A. (1987). Early social relationships: A psycho-biologist's view. *Child Development,* 48(3), 633-647.

Hoffman, M. (2002). Toward a comprehensive, empathy-based theory of moral development. In A. Bohart & D. Stipek, *Constructive and destructive behavior: Implications for family, school and society* (pp. 61-86). Washington, DC: American Psychological Association.

Hoover, J., & Oliver, R. (2008). *The bullying prevention handbook, 2nd Edition.* Bloomington, IN: Solution Tree.

Howell, J. (2007). Adventure boosts empowerment. *Reclaiming Children and Youth,* 16(1), 45-48.

Hubble, M., Duncan, B., & Miller, S. (1999). *The heart and soul of change.* Washington, DC: American Psychological Association.

Huttenlocher, P. R. (2002). *Neural plasticity: The effects of environment on the development of the cerebral cortex.* Cambridge, MA: Harvard University Press

Huxley, A. (1945). *The perennial philosophy.* New York: Harper and Row.

Hyman, I., & Snook, P. (1999). *Dangerous schools: What we can do about the physical and emotional abuse of our children.* San Francisco: Jossey-Bass.

Izard, C., & Ackerman, B. (2000). Motivational, organizational, and regulatory functions of discrete emotions. In M. Lewis & J. Haviland-Jones (Eds.), *Handbook of emotions (2nd edition)* (pp. 253-264). New York: Guilford.

Jenkins, R. (1958a). *Breaking patterns of defeat.* Philadelphia: J. B. Lippincott.

Jenkins, R. (1958b). Treatment considerations. In I. A. Weeks, *Youthful offenders at Highfields* (pp. 149-156). Ann Arbor: University of Michigan Press.

Johnson, S. (2004). *Mind wide open: Your brain and the neuroscience of everyday Life.* New York: Scribner.

Jung-Beeman, M. (2008). *Research: Solving problems with insight.* Downloaded February 15, 2008 from: http://www.psych.northwestern.edu/~mjungbee/research.htm

Juul, K. (1981). Cited in Brendtro, L. K., & Ness, A. E. (1983). *Re-educating troubled youth: Environments for teaching and treatment.* New York: Aldine de Gruyter.

Kagan, J. (2006). Cited in D. Goleman, *Social intelligence: The new science of human relationships.* London: Hutichinson.

Kagan, J. (1971). *Personality development.* New York: Harcourt Brace.

Kandel, E. (2006). *In search of memory.* New York: W. W. Norton Company.

Kandel, E. (2000). *The molecular biology of memory storage: A dialog between genes and synapses.* Nobel Lecture, December 8, 2000. Stockholm, Sweden.

Kardiner, A., & Spiegel, H. (1947). *War, stress and neurotic illness.* New York: Paul B. Hober.

Kauffman, J. (2000). Future directions with troubled children. *Reclaiming Children and Youth, 9*(2), 119-124.

Kazdin, A., & Weisz, J. (Eds.). (2003). *Evidence-based psychotherapies for children and adolescents.* New York: The Guilford Press.

Kellerman, J. (1999). *Savage spawn: Reflections on violent children.* New York: Ballantine.

Kevin C. (1994). My independence day. *Journal of Emotional and Behavioral Problems, 3*(2), 35-40.

Key, E. (1909). *The century of the child.* New York: G. P. Putnam's Sons.

Keyes, C. L. M., & Haidt, J. D. (2003). *Flourishing: Positive psychology and the life well-lived.* Washington, DC: American Psychological Association Press.

Khamisa, A. (2007). *From forgiveness to fulfillment.* La Jolla, CA: ANK Publishing.

Kloo, D., & Perner, J. (2008). Training theory of mind and executive control: A tool for improving school achievement. *Mind, Brain, and Education, 2*(3), 122-127.

Kluckhohn, C. (1949). *Mirror for man.* New York: McGraw Hill.

Koehler, N. (2006). Team planning to CLEAR up problems. *Reclaiming Children and Youth, 15*(3), 155-161.

Koltko-Rivera, M. (2006). Rediscovering the later version of Maslow's hierarchy of needs: Self-transcendence and opportunities for theory, research, and unification. *Review of General Psychology, 10* (2), 302-317.

Konner, M. (2002). *The tangled wing: Biological constraints on the human spirit (2nd ed.).* New York: Henry Holt and Company.

Krisberg, B. (2005). *Juvenile justice: Redeeming our children.* Thousand Oaks, CA: Sage Publications.

Lakhoff, G. (2004). *Don't think of an elephant: Know your values and frame the debate.* Melbourne: Scribe Publications.

Lantieri, L. (2001). An ounce of prevention is worth a pound of metal detectors. *Reclaiming Children and Youth,* 10(1), 33-38.

Laughlin, P., Hatch, E., Silver, J., & Boh, L. (2006). Groups perform better than the best individuals on letters-to-numbers problems: Effects of group size. *Journal of Personality and Social Psychology,* 90(4), 644-651.

Laursen, E. (2008). Respectful alliances. *Reclaiming Children and Youth,* 17(1), 4-9.

Lay, J. (2000). The person behind the file number. *Reclaiming Children and Youth,* 9(2), 68-69.

LeDoux, J. (2002). *Synaptic self: How our brains become who we are.* New York: Penguin Books.

Lewin, K. (1943/1999). The process of group living. In M. Gold (Ed.), *The complete social scientist: A Kurt Lewin reader* (pp. 333-348). Washington, DC: American Psychological Association.

Lewis, M. (1997). *Altering fate: Why the past does not predict the future.* New York: The Guilford Press.

Lewis, R. (2001). Classroom discipline and student responsibility: The students view. *Teaching and Teacher Education,* 17(3), 307-319.

Lewis, T., Amini, F., & Lannon, R. (2000). *A general theory of love.* New York: Random House.

Lippitt, R., & White, R. (1943). The "social climate" of children's groups. In R. Barker, J. Kounin, & H. Wright (Eds.), *Child behavior and development: A course of representative studies* (pp. 485-508). New York: McGraw-Hill.

Liss, S. (2006). *No place for children. Voices from juvenile detention.* Austin, TX: The University of Texas Press.

Lloyd, S., & Norfolk, S. (2007). You know too much. *Discover,* April, pp. 55-57.

Long, N., & Long, J. (2001). *The angry smile.* Austin, TX: PRO-ED.

Long, N., Morse, W., Fecser, F., & Newman, R. (2007). *Conflict in the classroom (6th ed.).* Austin, TX: PRO-ED. [previous editions published in 1965, 1971, 1976, 1980, and 1996.]

Long, N., Wood, M., & Fecser, F. (2001). *Life Space Crisis Intervention.* Austin, TX: Pro-ED Publishers.

Longhurst, J., & McCord, J. (2007). From peer deviance to peer helping. *Reclaiming Children and Youth,* 15(4), 194-199.

Lugo, W. (2006). Violent videogames recruit American youth. *Reclaiming Children and Youth,* 15(1), 11-14.

Lupien, S. (2004). The impact of socio-economic status on children's stress hormone levels: emotional processing and memory performance, audio recording, HDPT: www.fltwood.com/onsite/brain/2004april/03.shtml cited in Cooper & Jobe, 2007.

Lynam, D. (1998). Early identification of the fledging psychopath: Locating the psychopathic child in the current nomenclature. *Journal of Abnormal Psychology*, 107(4), 566-575.

Lynam, D. (1997). Pursuing the psychopath: Capturing the fledgling psychopath in a nomological net. *Journal of Abnormal Psychology*, 106(2), 425-438.

MacLean, P. (1990). *The triune brain in evolution*. New York: Plenum Press.

Maczkowiack, H. (2006). *An awkward fit*. Adelaide: Open Book Australia.

Malinowski, B. (1960 [1944]). *A scientific theory of culture and other essays*. New York: Oxford University Press.

Mandela, N. (2003). A fabric of care. In K. Asmal, D. Chidester, & W. James (Eds.), *Nelson Mandela: From freedom to the future* (pp. 416-418). Johannesburg: Jonathan Ball Publishers.

Markovitch, S., Jacques, S., Boseovski, J., & Zelazo, P. (2008). Self-reflection and the cognitive control of behavior: Implications for learning. *Mind, Brain, and Education*, 2(3), 122-127.

Marshall, C. (2004). Emergence. *Reclaiming Children and Youth*, 13(1), 14-15.

Martin, F., & Osgood, D. W. (1987). Autonomy as a source of pro-social influence among incarcerated adolescents. *Journal of Applied Social Psychology*, 17(2), 97-107.

Martini, M., & Kirkpatrick, J. (1992). Parenting in Polynesia: A view from the Marquesas. In J. K.Roopnarine & D. B. Carter (Eds.), *Parent-child socialization in diverse cultures, Vol. 5* (pp. 199-222). Norwood, NJ: Ablex Publishers.

Martinson, R. (1974). What works? Questions and answers about prison reform. *The Public Interest*, 10, 22-54.

Maslow, A. (1970). *Motivation and personality*. New York: Harper Row.

McCall, H. (2003). When successful alternative students "disengage" from regular school. *Reclaiming Children and Youth*, 12(2), 113-117.

McCorkle, L., Elias, A., & Bixby, F. (1958). *The Highfields story: An experimental treatment project for youthful offenders*. New York: Henry Holt and Company.

McCullough, M., Kilpatrick, S., Emmons, R., & Larson, D. (2001). Is gratitude a moral affect? *Psychological Bulletin*, 127(2), 249-256.

McDermott, J. (2004). Evolution of a journal. *Child and Adolescent Psychiatry*, 43(6), 650-659.

McDougal, W. (1920). *The group mind*. New York: G. P. Putnam's Sons.

Menninger, K. (1963). *The vital balance: The life process in mental health and illness.* New York: The Viking Press.

Merker, B. (2007). Consciousness without a cerebral cortex: A challenge for neuroscience and medicine. *Behavioral and Brain Sciences, 30*(1), 63-81.

Mikulincer, M., Shaver, P., Gillath, O., & Nitzberg, R. (2005). Attachment, caregiving, and altruism: Boosting attachment security increases compassion and helping. *Journal of Personal and Social Psychology, 89*(5), 817-839.

Miller, W. R., & Rollnick, S. (1991). *Motivational interviewing: Preparing people to change addictive behavior.* New York: The Guilford Press.

Mitchell, M. (2003). The million dollar child. *Reclaiming Children and Youth, 12*(1), 6-8.

Mitchell, O., & McKenzie, D. (2006). The stability of resilience and self-control in a sample of incarcerated offenders. *Crime & Delinquency, 52*(3), 432-439.

Mizushima, K., & Jenkins, R. (1962). Treatment needs corresponding to varieties of delinquents. *International Journal of Social Psychology, 8*(91), 91-103.

Moffitt, T. (2003). Adolescence-limited and life-course-specific antisocial behavior: A developmental taxonomy. *Psychological Review, 100*(4), 674-701.

Moll, J., Krueger, F., Zahn, R., Pardini, M., de Oliveira-Souza, R., & Grafman, J. (2006). Human fronto-mesolimbic networks guide decisions about charitable donation. *Proceedings of the National Academies of the Sciences [PNAS]* 103(42), 15623-15628. Available online at: www.pnas.org/cgi/doi/10.1073/pnas.0604475103

Moos, R. H. (1979). *Evaluating educational environments: Procedures, measures, findings, and policy implications.* San Francisco: Jossey-Bass.

Moos, R. H. (1974). *Evaluating treatment environments: A social ecological approach.* New York: John Wiley & Sons.

Morse, W. C. (2008). *Connecting with kids in conflict: A life space legacy.* Sioux Falls, SD: Reclaiming Children and Youth & Starr Commonwealth.

Morse, W. C. (1985). *The education and treatment of socioemotionally impaired children and youth.* Syracuse, NY: Syracuse University Press.

Morse, W. C. (1974). Cover copy to H. Vorrath & L. Brendtro, *Positive Peer Culture.* Chicago: Aldine Publishing Company.

Morse, W. C., Cutler, R., & Fink, A. (1964). *Public school classes for emotionally disturbed children: A research analysis.* Washington, DC: Council for Exceptional Children.

Mullin, B., & Hinshaw, S. (2007). Emotional regulation and externalizing emotions in children and adolescents. In J. Gross (Ed.), *Handbook of emotion regulation* (pp. 523-541). New York: The Guilford Press.

Murray, H. (1938). *Explorations into personality.* New York: Oxford University Press.

Myers, J. (2007). Restraints that kill. *Youth Today,* 95, pp. 1, 21-23.

Neath, I., & Surprenant, A. (2003). *Human memory.* Belmont, CA: Wadsworth.

Nelson, E. E., & Panksepp, J. (1998). Brain substrates of infant-mother attachments: Contributions of opiates, oxytocin, and norepinephrine. *Neuroscience and Behavioral Reviews,* 22, 437-452.

Neufeld, G., & Maté, G. (2005). *Hold on to your kids: Why parents need to matter more than peers.* New York: Ballantine Books.

Newkirk, R., & Rutstein, N. (2000). *Racial healing: The Institutes for Healing Racism.* Albion, MI: Starr Commonwealth.

Newman, J. P. (1998). Psychopathic behavior and information processing perspective. In D. J. Cook, A. E. Forth, & R. D. Hare (Eds.), *Psychopathy: Theory, research, and implications for society* (pp. 81-104). Dordecht, Netherlands: Kluwer.

Nichols, J. G. (1990). What is ability and why we are mindful of it. In R. J. Sternberg, & J. Kolligian, Jr. *Competence considered* (pp. 11-40). New Haven, NJ: Yale University Press.

Nichols, J. G. (1984). Conceptions of ability and achievement motivation. In R. Ames & C. Ames (Eds.), *Research on motivation in education* (Vol. 1, pp. 39-73). New York: Academic Press.

Nietzsche, F. W. (1897). *Essay on genealogy of morals,* essay 2, aphorism 15.

NIH. (2007). Brain matures a few years later in ADHD but follows normal pattern. *National Institute of Health Science News,* November 12. www.nimh.nih.gov/science-news/2007

Nisbett, R., & Cohen, D. (1996). *Culture of honor: The psychology of violence in the South.* Boulder, CO: Westview Press.

Nissen, L. (2006). Bringing strength-based philosophy to life in juvenile justice. *Reclaiming Children and Youth,* 15, 40-46.

Odney, J., & Brendtro, L. (1992). Students grade their schools. *Journal of Emotional and Behavioral Problems,* 1(1), 4-9.

Olive, E. (2008). *Positive Behavior Facilitation.* Champaign, IL: Research Press.

Opp, G., Unger, N., & Teichmann, J. (2007). Together, not alone: Positive Peer Culture in a German school. *Reclaiming Children and Youth,* 15(4), 234-242.

Osgood, D. W., & Briddell, L. (2006). Peer effects and juvenile justice. In K. Dodge, T. Dishion, & J. Lansford (Eds.), *Deviant peer influences in programs for youth* (pp. 141-161). New York: The Guilford Press.

Osgood, D. W., Gruber, E., Archer, M., & Newcomb, T. (1985). Autonomy for inmates: Counter culture or co-option? *Criminal Justice and Behavior,* 12(1), 71-89.

Packard, E. (2007). That teenage feeling. *Monitor on Psychology,* 38(4), 20-22.

Perry, B., & Hambrick, E. (2008). An introduction to the neurosequential model of therapeutics. *Reclaiming Children and Youth,* 17(3), 38-43.

Perry, B., & Szalavitz, M. (2006). *The boy who was raised as a dog. What traumatized children can teach us about love, loss, and healing.* New York: Basic Books.

Pestalozzi, J. H (1801). *How Gertrude teaches her children.* Translated 1915. Syracuse, NY: W. Bardeen.

Peterson, C. (2008). *The strength-based revolution.* Presentation to the Roots and Wings Conference, Reclaiming Youth International, Wayne State University, Detroit, MI, Sept. 20, 2008.

Peterson, C., Maier, S., & Seligman, M. (1993). *Learned helplessness: A theory for the age of control.* New York: Oxford University Press.

Peterson, C., Park, N., & Sweeney, P. (2008). Group well-being: Morale from a positive psychology perspective. *Applied Psychology: An International Review,* 57, 19-36.

Peterson, C., & Seligman, M. (2004). *Character strengths and virtues: A handbook for classification.* Washington, DC: American Psychological Association.

Peter, V. (1999). *What makes Boys Town succeed?* Boys Town, NE: Boys Town Press.

Phelan, J. (2004). Some thoughts on using an ecosystem perspective. *CYC-Online,* Issue 28. www.cyc-net.org.

Polsky, H. (1962.) *Cottage Six. The social system of delinquent boys in residential treatment.* New York: Wiley.

Polsky, H., & Berger, R. (2002). *From custodialism to community: A theory-based manual for transforming institutions.* Lanham, MD: University Press of America.

Provine, R. (2000). *Laughter: A scientific investigation.* New York: Penguin Books.

Purkey, W. W. (1970). *Self-concept and school achievement.* Englewood Cliffs, NJ: Prentice-Hall.

Quay, H. C. (1987). Patterns of delinquent behavior. In H. C. Quay (Ed.), *Handbook of juvenile delinquency* (pp. 118-138). New York: John Wiley.

Quigley, R. (2007). Positive Peer Culture: Harry Vorrath – The man and the myth. *Reclaiming Children and Youth,* 15(4), 207-209.

Quigley, R. (2004). Positive peer culture groups: Helping others meets primary developmental needs. *Reclaiming Children and Youth, 13*(3), 134-137.

Radio Lab. (April 28, 2006). Chimp Fights and Trolley Rides. www.wnyc.org/shows/radiolab/episodes/2006/04/28/segments

Ratey, J. J. (2002). *A user's guide to the brain: Perception, attention, and the four theaters of the brain.* New York: Vintage Books.

Rawls, J. (2002). *Justice as fairness.* Cambridge, MA: Belknap, Harvard University Press.

Redl, F. (1966). *When we deal with children.* New York: Free Press.

Redl, F., & Wineman, D. (1957). *The aggressive child.* Glencoe, IL: Free Press.

Reinke, W., & Walker, H. (2006). Deviant peer effects in education. In K. Dodge, T. Dishion, & J. Lansford, (Eds.), *Deviant peer influences in programs for youth: Problems and solutions* (pp. 122-140). New York: Guilford Press.

Reyna, V., & Farley, F. (2006). Risk and rationality in adolescent decision making: Implications for theory, practice, and public policy. *Psychological Science in the Public Interest, 7*(1), entire issue, pp. 1-44.

Rios, T. (1997). Growing up in prison. *Reclaiming Children and Youth, 6*(3), 136-137.

Rizzolatti, G., Fadiga, L., Gallese, V., & Fogassi, L. (1996). Pre-motor cortex and the recognition of motor actions. *Cognitive Brain Research, 3*(2), 131-141.

Rogoff, B. (2003). *The cultural nature of human development.* New York: Oxford University Press.

Ross, A. (2007). Transformation education: Revisiting the therapeutic milieu to harness the power of culture. *Reclaiming Children and Youth, 16*(3), 5-9.

Ross, A., Grenier, G., & Kros, F. (2005). *Creating the upside down organization: Transforming staff to save troubled children.* Baltimore: Children's Guild.

Sapolsky, R. (2002). *A primate's memoir: A neuroscientist's unconventional life among the baboons.* New York: Touchstone.

Schoof, K. (1993). Our minds just can't feel happy. *Journal of Emotional and Behavioral Problems, 2*(2), 5-9.

Schorr, A. N. (1994). *Affect regulation and origin of the self: The neurobiology of emotional development.* Hillsdale, NJ: Earlbaum.

Schwartz, I. M., & Fishman, G. (1999). *Kids raised by the government.* Westport, CT: Praeger.

Seita, J., & Brendtro, L. (2005). *Kids who outwit adults.* Bloomington, IN: Solution Tree.

Seita, J., Mitchell, M., & Tobin, C. (1996). *In whose best interest. One child's odyssey, a nation's responsibility.* Elizabethtown, PA: Continental Press.

Seligman, M., & Czikszentmihalyi, M. (2000). Positive psychology: An introduction. *American Psychologist,* 55(1), 5-14.

Shamay-Tsoory, S., Tomer, R., & Aharon-Peretz, J. (2005). The neuroanatomical basis of understanding sarcasm and its relation to social cognition. *Neuropsychology,* 19(3), 288-300.

Siegel, D. (2006). An interpersonal neurobiology approach to psychotherapy. *Psychiatric Annals,* 36(4), 248-256.

Skinner, B. F. (1971). *Beyond freedom and dignity.* New York: Alfred A. Knopf.

Skinner, B. F. (1964, May 21). Education in 1984. *New Scientist,* 484.

Smith, L. (2004). A retrospective review of The Aggressive Child: An early and major exemplar of qualitative inquiry. *Qualitative Social Work,* 3(2), 221-231.

Sperber, D., & Wilson, D. (1986). *Relevance: Communication and cognition.* Oxford, UK: Basil Blackwell.

Sroufe, L. A., Egeland, B., Carlson, E. A., & Collins, W. A. (2005). *The development of the person: The Minnesota study of risk and adaptation from birth to childhood.* New York: The Guilford Press.

Starr Commonwealth. (1999). *Treatment environmental survey.* Albion, MI: Starr Commonwealth Training Resource Center.

Steele, W. (2008). Clinician or witness? The intervener's relationship with traumatized children. *Reclaiming Children and Youth,* 17(3), 44-47.

Steinberg, L., & Cauffman, E. (1996). Maturity of judgment in adolescents: Psychosocial factors in adolescent decision making. *Law and Human Behavior,* 20(3), 249-272.

Sternberg, R. (1996). *Successful intelligence: How practical and creative intelligence determines success in life.* New York: Simon and Schuster.

Sternberg, R. J., & Kolligian, J., Jr. (1990a). Preface. *Competence considered* (pp. ix-xv). New Haven, NJ: Yale University Press.

Sternberg, R. J., & Kolligian, J., Jr. (1990b). *Competence considered.* New Haven, NJ: Yale University Press.

Storm Trooper Steve. (1996). Conflicts of the heart. *Reclaiming Children and Youth,* 5(3), 126-127.

Stott, D. (1950/1980). *Delinquency and human nature.* [Second edition, 1980.] London: Hodder and Stoughton.

Strother, M. (2007). A mind for adventure. *Reclaiming Children and Youth,* 16(1), 17-21.

Stürmer, S., Snyder, M., & Omoto, A. (2005). Prosocial emotions and helping: The moderating role of group membership. *Journal of Personality and Social Psychology,* 88(3), 532-546.

Sue, D. W., Capodilupo, C., Torino, G. C., Buccerí, J. M., Holder, A., Nadal, K., & Esquiln, M. (2007). Racial microaggressions in everyday life. *American Psychologist,* 62(4), 271-286.

Sylwester, R. (2005). *How to explain a brain.* Thousand Oaks, CA: Corwin Press.

Tancredi, L. (2005). *Hardwired behavior: What neuroscience reveals about reality.* New York: Cambridge University Press.

Tangey, J. P. (2001). Constructive and destructive aspects of shame and guilt. In A. C. Bohart & D. J. Stipek (Eds.), *Constructive & destructive behavior: Implications for family, school, and society* (pp. 127-145). Washington, DC: American Psychological Association.

Tate, T., & Wasmund, W. (2000). *Partners in empowerment: A peer group primer.* Albion, MI; Starr Commonwealth

Taylor, J., Gilligan, C., & Sullivan, A. (1996). What gets me into trouble is "my big mouth!!": Women and girls, race and relationship. *Reclaiming Children and Youth,* 5(2), 68-73.

Taylor, S. (2002). *The tending instinct: How nurturing is essential to who we are and how we live.* New York: Holt.

Taylor, S., & Gonzaga, G. (2007). Affilliative responses to stress: A social neuroscience model. In E. Harmon-Jones & P. Winkielman (Eds.), *Social neuroscience: Integrating biological and psychological explanations of social behavior* (pp. 454-473). New York: The Guilford Press.

Tileston, D. W. (2006). Self-efficacy. In S. Feinstein (Ed.), *The Praeger Handbook of Learning and the Brain, Vol. 2* (pp. 431-434). Westport, CT: Praeger Publications.

Toch, H., & Adams, K. (2002). *Acting out: Maladaptive behavior in confinement.* Washington, DC: American Psychological Association.

Tompkins-Rosenblat, P., & VanderVen, K. (2005). Perspectives on point and level systems in residential care: A responsive dialogue. *Residential Treatment for Children and Youth,* 22(3), 1-18.

Trieschman, A., Whittaker, J., & Brendtro, L. (1969). *The other 23 hours.* Chicago: Aldine.

Twenge, J., Baumeister, R., DeWall, C. N., Ciarocco, N., & Bartles, J. N. (2007). Social exclusion decreases prosocial behavior. *Journal of Personality and Social Psychology,* 92(1), 56-66.

Valore, T. (2007). Creating cohesive groups in Re-ED. In R. Cantrell & M. Cantrell (Eds.), *Helping troubled children and youth* (pp. 299-321). Memphis, TN: American Re-education Association.

van der Kolk, B., McFarlane, A., & Weisaeth, L. (2007). *Traumatic stress: The effects of overwhelming experience on mind, body, and society.* New York: Guilford Press.

van der Kolk, B. (2005). Developmental trauma disorder: Towards a rational diagnosis for children with complex trauma histories. *Psychiatric Annals,* 33(5), 401-408.

VanderVen, K. (ed.) (2009). Controls from within. *Special issue, Reclaiming Children and Youth,* 17(4).

VanderVen, K. (2003). Transforming the milieu and lives through the power of activity: Theory and practice. *Journal of Child and Youth Care Work,* 19:103-108.

Vilikazi, H. (1993). Rediscovering lost truths. *Reclaiming Children and Youth,* 1(4), 37.

Vorrath, H. & Brendtro, L. (1985). *Positive Peer Culture (2nd Ed.).* Piscataway, NJ: Transaction Publishers, Rutgers University.

Vygotsky, L. S. (2003). Cited in K. VanderVen, Transforming the milieu and lives through the power of activity: Theory and practice. *Journal of Child and Youth Care Work,* 19: 103-108.

Vygotsky, L. S. (1971). *Denken und Sprechen* (3rd Auflage). Frankfurt/M.: Fischer.

Wachtel, T. (2003). Restorative justice in everyday life: Beyond the ritual. *Reclaiming Children and Youth,* 12(2), 82-87. For further resources, see the website of the International Institute for Restorative Practices, www.iirp.org

Walsh, F. (2006). *Strengthening family resilience* (2nd Ed). New York: The Guilford Press.

Warneken, F., & Thomasello, M. (2006, March 3). Altruistic helping in young infants. *Science,* 311(5765) 1301-1303.

Wasmund, W. (1988). The social climates of peer group and other residential programs. *Child and Youth Care Quarterly,* 17(3), 146-155.

Wasmund, W., & Tate, T. (2000). *Partners in empowerment.* Albion, MI: Starr Commonwealth.

Watson, J. (2002). Cited in M. Konner, *The tangled wing: Biological constraints on the human spirit* (2nd ed.). New York: Henry Holt and Company.

Way, D. (1993). I just have a half heart. *Journal of Emotional and Behavioral Problems,* 2(1), 4-5.

Weeks, H. A. (1958). *Youthful offenders at Highfields: An evaluation of the effects of short-term treatment of delinquent boys.* Ann Arbor: The University of Michigan Press.

Weisz, J., & Hawley, K. (2002). Developmental factors in the treatment of adolescents. *Journal of Consulting and Clinical Psychology,* 70(1), 21-43.

Werner, E., & Smith, R. (1992). *Overcoming the odds.* Ithaca, NY: Cornell University Press.

Wexler, B. (2006). *Brain and culture: Neurobiology, ideology, and social change.* Cambridge, MA: MIT Press.

Whewell, W. (1847). *The philosophy of the inductive sciences.* London: Parker.

White, R. (1959). Motivation reconsidered. The concept of competence. *Psychological Review,* 66: 297-313.

White, R., & Lippitt, R. (1960). *Autocracy and democracy: An experimental inquiry.* New York: Harper.

Wilson, E. O. (1998). *Consilience: The unity of knowledge.* New York: Alfred A. Knopf.

Wineman, D. (1960). *Book reviews: Youthful Offenders at Highfields.* Social Work, XX, p. 120.

Wolins, M., & Wosner, Y. (1982). *Revitalizing residential settings: Problems and potential in education, health, rehabilitation, and social service.* San Francisco: Jossey-Bass.

Woodland Hills Students. (1993). I lost everything. *Journal of Emotional and Behavioral Problems,* 2(3), 5-7.

Wozner, Y. (1982). Assessing the quality of internat life. *Human Relations,* 35(11), 1059-1072.

Yalom, I. (1995). *The theory and practice of group psychotherapy* (4th ed.). New York: Basic Books.

Yeibio, L. (2007, November 22). Infants exhibit early understanding of social behavior. *Nature,* 450: 557-559.

Zak, P. J. (Ed.). (2008). *Moral markets: The critical role of values in the economy.* Princeton, NJ: Princeton University Press.

Zeigarnik, B. (1927). Das Behalten von erledigten und unerledigten Handlungen. [The memory of completed and uncompleted tasks.] *Psychologische Forschung,* 9: 1-85.

INDEX